Climate Change and the Future of Boston

Anthem Environment and Sustainability Initiative

The **Anthem Environment and Sustainability** book series seeks to push the frontiers of scholarship while simultaneously offering prescriptive and programmatic advice to policymakers and practitioners around the world. The programme publishes research monographs, professional and major reference works, upper-level textbooks and general interest titles.

Series Editor
Professor Lawrence Susskind
MIT

Included within the AESI is the Anthem EnviroExperts Review. Through this an online micro-review site, Anthem Press seeks to build a community of practice involving scientists, policy analysts and activists committed to creating a clearer and deeper understanding of how ecological systems—at every level—operate, and how they have been damaged by unsustainable development. This site publishes short reviews of important books or reports in the environmental field, broadly defined.

Visit the site at: http://www.anthemenviroexperts.com.

Climate Change and the Future of Boston

Courtney Humphries

ANTHEM PRESS

Anthem Press
An imprint of Wimbledon Publishing Company
www.anthempress.com

This edition first published in UK and USA 2027
by ANTHEM PRESS
75–76 Blackfriars Road, London SE1 8HA, UK
or PO Box 9779, London SW19 7ZG, UK
and
244 Madison Ave #116, New York, NY 10016, USA

First published in the UK and USA by Anthem Press in 2026

British Library Cataloguing-in-Publication Data
A catalogue record for this book is available from the British Library.

Library of Congress Cataloging-in-Publication Data: 2026951131
A catalog record for this book has been requested.

ISBN-13: 978-1-80136-056-2 (Pbk)
ISBN-10: 1-80136-056-1 (Pbk)

Cover credit: Courtney Humphries

This title is also available as an eBook.

CONTENTS

LIST OF FIGURES

ACKNOWLEDGMENTS

This book represents many years of following Boston's response to climate change, which I have approached as a journalist, a researcher, and a concerned resident of the city of more than two decades. The project was informed by many discussions over the years with city officials, academics, urban planners, architects, non-profit representatives, journalists, community members, and others involved in climate issues in Boston, and I am grateful for these conversations. I was guided by the insight of the faculty at the University of Massachusetts Boston School for the Environment where I began this project as a PhD student, particularly my advisors John Duff and Alan Wiig; dissertation committee members Paul Kirshen, Bob Chen, and Elizabeth Hamin; as well as other faculty whose input helped guide my work, including Ellen Douglas, Antonio Raciti, and Rosalyn Negrón. As a Visiting Assistant Professor at Boston College, I benefited from the support of the Core Curriculum under the leadership of Elizabeth Shlala. This manuscript was shaped and improved through the input of series editors, the Anthem Editorial staff, and the thoughtful comments of anonymous reviewers, and I am grateful for their help in bringing this project to fruition. Finally, I'm incredibly thankful for the support of my family, and particularly my husband Theodore Stocker and daughter Juniper Stories.

Chapter 1

INTRODUCTION: A CITY IN TRANSITION

Until recently, climate change was generally discussed as a future threat to cities in North America. Even in cities leading the way on reducing emissions of greenhouse gases responsible for global warming and planning for the impacts of climate change, the risks were often described as years or decades away. Today, however, cities increasingly find themselves embedded within an environment that is already rapidly changing. Heat waves, wildfires, flooding, and storm damage are becoming more common and more expensive; the United States experiences a weather-related extreme event costing a billion dollars or more every three weeks (up from every four months in the 1980s) (U.S. Global Change Research Program 2023). Recent developments highlight the urgency of climate action, both for mitigating climate change by reducing greenhouse gas emission and for adapting to the impacts. After a brief global slowing of emissions due to the COVID-19 pandemic, emissions have continued to rise, according to the International Monetary Fund Climate Change Dashboard. The most recent Intergovernmental Panel on Climate Change (IPCC) report, AR6, describes "a rapidly closing window of opportunity to secure a livable and sustainable future for all" (IPCC 2022, 29). It finds that we are likely to cross a threshold of 1.5°C in average warming (which is backed up by recent research) and dramatic emissions reductions are needed to limit warming below 2°C, which could have dire impacts on agriculture, health, and other systems around the world.

Recent assessments of climate change underscore three important points. First, climate change appears to be rapidly intensifying; climate-related impacts are becoming more widespread, severe, or frequent. Second, urban areas continue to play a critical role in addressing the challenge of climate change, as they are responsible for more than two-thirds of global greenhouse gas emissions. Urban areas are also home to a growing proportion of the world's population, and they are places where climate risks and impacts tend to concentrate as the built environment exacerbates extreme heat, flooding, pollution, and other climate-related risks. Third, mitigating and adapting to climate change will involve transformative societal actions that have wide-ranging social, environmental, and economic consequences. Urban climate governance is increasingly focused on pursuing low-carbon futures (Bulkeley 2010) and just urban transitions that reduces emissions while addressing inequities in climate vulnerabilities and the environmental benefits of climate mitigation and adaptation actions (Hughes and Hoffmann 2020). These points underscore a need to understand how cities and metropolitan areas are experiencing and planning for climate change, how they are implementing policies addressing climate mitigation and adaptation, how they are governing just transitions, and where they are failing to meet those goals. Ultimately, it also requires understanding whether and how the targeted policies of individual cities can scale upward and outward to a broader societal change (Heijden 2023).

This book provides an in-depth case study of Boston, Massachusetts, as it seeks to mitigate and adapt to climate change. It is part of a series dedicated to exploring North American cities in detail, drawing on the framework of the Urban Climate Change Research Network (UCCRN), a consortium of over 1,200 people in over 150 cities worldwide working on providing an urban perspective on climate change mitigation and adaptation. The UCCRN has organized three major Assessment Reports on Climate Change and Cities (ARC3) that have been a wide-reaching effort to create an interdisciplinary, global, science-based assessment of urban climate action across the world, and it sponsors a database of shorter case studies of urban responses to climate change. Case studies are essential for bringing empirical evidence and lived nuance to broader theories about climate mitigation, adaptation, and governance. This extended, book-length case study allows for a comprehensive and in-depth view of climate change on a local level.

Why focus on Boston? Boston has a long track record of science-based climate policy, and it is among the cities consistently working to reduce its carbon footprint. It has set a goal of carbon neutrality by 2050. And it has a reduced citywide emissions by 21% and per capita emissions by 40% from 2005 to 2019 (City of Boston Environment Department 2021) in spite of population growth, economic growth, and intense real estate development in many areas of the city. It has created one of the country's most ambitious regulations to track and regulate greenhouse gas emissions from major buildings and has created a first-of-its kind policy to require net zero emissions in new buildings, one of the major sources of carbon pollution in the city.

At the same time, Boston faces challenges shared by coastal communities, which collectively are home to 40% of the U.S. population (U.S. Global Change

Research Program 2023). Based on the city's sea-level rise projects, one-fifth of Boston's land could be flooded in a major storm (1% annual chance) by late this century, and 5% of its land could be flooded with monthly high tides. It also faces a growing frequency and length of extreme heat events, a public health challenge for a city where many residents lack air conditioning. Although the city has not yet been hit by major climate-change-related disasters, Boston has taken climate adaptation seriously; over the past decade, the city has engaged in public planning processes that have brought attention to neighborhood-level risks and vulnerabilities and made climate change a high-profile concern. Boston has taken a deliberate and science-based approach to adaptation, collecting locally relevant data about climate impacts and vulnerabilities to inform planning and policy. Its municipal government has been engaging in detailed planning for climate risks related to sea-level rise for the past decade, putting it alongside New York, Miami, San Francisco, Norfolk, and Charleston as a leader in planning infrastructure in an era of accelerating sea levels and storms. It has implemented innovative regulations to make buildings in floodplains more resilient. It has also created recent plans for managing extreme heat and improving its green infrastructure and urban forest to offset the impacts of heat and stormwater flooding. All of this is remarkable given the fact that Boston has not yet been hit by a devastating climate-related disaster. Its proactive and science-based approach to climate adaptation, made possible by broad political support and an enviable educational infrastructure, has put Boston at the forefront of anticipatory planning for climate impacts.

While Boston has long been a champion of climate action, its strategies have evolved over time. Beginning with limited policy experiments to promote sustainability, the city has gradually expanded its ambitions and its capacity to address climate change. With the election of Michelle Wu in 2021, Boston became one of a small number of cities to embrace the Green New Deal (GND), a platform that seeks to integrate climate change, job creation, and social and economic inequity. As cities begin to increasingly seek to address social justice and equity in climate action, Boston, long a climate champion, has also become an important test case for urban policy centered on a climate justice framework. Its broader policy evolution offers an opportunity to understand how cities move from measuring greenhouse gases and making commitments to pursuing a just transition toward equitable carbon neutrality.

Climate change requires cities to orient their governance toward the future in ways that they did not in the past. Robust climate governance at a local scale requires collecting data about the state of the system, projections of climate change impacts, and metrics for evaluating the city's progress along climate-related goals. The UCCRN's second assessment report,

ARC3.2, describes five "pathways to urban transformation" through which cities are successfully taking climate action. These pathways can be seen as a set of best practices based on an analysis of the adaptation and mitigation actions of 100 cities around the world. The pathways are: (1) integrating mitigation and adaptation, (2) integrating disaster risk reduction and climate adaptation into urban development, (3) creating plans that are inclusive and co-generated with a variety of stakeholders and experts, (4) embedding equity and justice into long-term planning and policymaking, and (5) building their own capacities by developing diverse sources of financing for climate action and participating in national and international networks. In Boston, we can see examples of efforts by municipal leaders to pursue all these pathways. While described as mutually inclusive actions that should be pursued simultaneously, tradeoffs do emerge. For example, the pursuit of financing for climate change solutions—particularly private investment and efforts to build a city's overall financial capacity—can complicate goals of pursuing equity and environmental justice.

Today, Boston is a growing city with newly redeveloped neighborhoods, world-class universities, a strong economy, and a recent history of revenue growth. The city has been harnessing these advantages as it seeks to understand its climate impacts and risks, and to marshal numerous stakeholders and strategies to mitigate and adapt to climate change. But the city also faces challenges to meeting the ambitious goals it has set. Boston has benefitted from statewide trends in cleaner energy, for instance, and will need to make more transformative changes to continue its downward emissions trajectory. It must rein in emissions from large institutional buildings and faces the daunting task of retrofitting its historic building stock. It must find ways to lower transportation emissions while contending with an aged and inequitable public transportation network and political challenges at the state and local level. Boston struggles to integrate a progressive vision of itself as a resilient and equitable city with a history of serving elite interests in the pursuit of economic growth, private investment, and real estate development. Consequently, the city's efforts to improve climate mitigation and adaptation are often embedded within development processes that leave out some of its residents—or force those residents to leave. Meanwhile, Boston is also suffering from a post-COVID decline in new development and an economy that is highly dependent on higher education and federal research funding, both currently challenged by federal government actions under the Trump administration. The city and metropolitan region may need to innovate further in generating local funding capacity to achieve its near-term goals.

ARC3.2 acknowledged that the potential of cities to "respond to climate change with transformative solutions of global significance" had so far been met with mostly "incremental" actions (Rosenzweig et al. 2018, 5). Climate-forward cities that were quick to set ambitious goals have struggled to meet specific performance targets (Markolf et al. 2020). Municipal governments are often constrained in their ability to meet targets based on political realities and the tools at their disposal; they must work within the legal and regulatory frameworks of state and federal government, and often with very limited financing to build new climate-resilient infrastructure. Still, cities, regions, businesses and other institutions have a critical role to play in meeting global greenhouse gas reduction goals, particularly in the United States where federal action and policy have been uneven (Kuramochi et al. 2020).

Boston's history of climate action certainly provides examples of incrementalism. Later in this book, I characterize this approach as a "climate mechanic" view of climate policy, drawing on the city's influential former mayor Thomas H. Menino, who often referred to himself as an "urban mechanic" in his approach to fixing urban problems. Cities today must shift from functioning as mechanics to becoming system designers and change facilitators. They must shepherd broader changes in urban energy systems, transportation, and infrastructure to make cities fossil-fuel free and prepared to thrive in a changing climate. And they must do so in a way that engages and values the perspectives of historically marginalized groups and people with greater social vulnerabilities. A case study of Boston is an opportunity to understand the nuances of these dynamics. Boston provides a concrete example of how cities can work to accelerate climate action and engage in just transitions within constraints that limit municipal action. The success Boston's GND will depend on its continued political support. Despite growing hostility at the federal level to both climate change and social justice issues, Wu is set to handily win a reelection in 2025, ensuring that her climate agenda will continue to move forward on a local level.

The UCCRN's third assessment report, ARC3.3, is still in development at the time of this writing, so this book cannot engage with its larger framework, though it is influenced by my participation as a co-author in the Governance Element, as well as early published sections of ARC3.3. It is clear that the understanding of climate mitigation and adaptation in cities has deepened greatly over the past few years as scholarship and perspectives have expanded, and as we have learned more about cities' response to urban challenges through the recent pandemic and escalating climate crisis. ARC3.3 includes a greater emphasis on issues of social equity and justice for vulnerable populations, in keeping with a growing awareness of the uneven nature of climate risks, impacts, and responses. For this reason, I have placed equity alongside mitigation and adaptation as one of the major pillars of climate action.

ARC3.2 describes cities as "complex social-ecological systems (SES)" that contain social and ecological components interacting dynamically at multiple spatial and temporal scales (Rosenzweig et al. 2018, 7). But it also recognizes technology as a "profound" influence in shaping the "structure, metabolism, and management of cities" and sees the "integration of social, ecological, and technological system in cities" as a potential catalyst of transformative responses to climate change (Rosenzweig et al. 2018, 7–8). Given this framing, I will extend the concept of an SES to the more recently developed conceptualization of urban environments as social, ecological and technological systems (SETS) in exploring climate change in Boston. SETS research offers a holistic perspective on urban systems that overcomes limitations to previous framings that focus on socio-technological interactions while ignoring ecology, or on social–ecological interactions while ignoring the role of technology and infrastructure in shaping system dynamics, including the potential for transforming systems for greater sustainability and resilience (McPhearson et al. 2021a). Urban systems are inherently relational and emergent. Distinct elements of social, ecological and technological domains are coupled and impact one another, often in a bi- or multi-directional manner. Climate-related shocks and stresses may impact the social, ecological, and technological domains in different ways (Chang et al. 2021). This perspective highlights how infrastructure decisions can lock in particular pathways, increasing the overall fragility of an urban system (Markolf et al. 2018), but it also opens up possibilities to reimagine infrastructure and its transformational role in sustainable urban futures (Grabowski et al. 2017). The SETS perspective is useful for studying urban climate transitions, because they require significant investment in new and retrofitted infrastructure. Understanding how infrastructure investments are shaped by social and ecological systems—and in turn shape them—could help guide better decision-making for a changing climate. This is particularly true given the widespread interest in green and nature-based infrastructure for climate adaptation in Boston and other cities—often designed for both ecological and social co-benefits—that exemplifies the interdependence of social, ecological, and infrastructural aspects of sustainable cities. While the SETS framework has its origins in urban ecosystem science, it shares connections with interdisciplinary research in SES and critical scholarship on sociotechnical systems, which have developed parallel conceptual understandings of technology as "a mediator of human-environment relationships" (Ahlborg et al. 2019, 2). Engaging with critical and conceptual fields can be an important counterbalance to positivist views of urban SETS that overlook questions of power in the ontological and epistemological framings of urban system dynamics and their solutions.

This book has four following chapters, which are organized as follows. Chapter 2 describes Boston's current carbon footprint and its projected impacts in a changing climate, focusing on sea-level rise, precipitation, and heat. Chapter 3 places Boston's climate picture within a historical context, drawing on the SETS framework to consider how historical urban development shapes the city's current challenges and opportunities in responding to climate change. Chapter 4 focuses on the recent evolution and current state of climate action planning in Boston's municipal government. Chapter 5 considers the multilevel governance of climate action in Boston, including municipal, regional, state, and federal government and the broader network of non-governmental actors that shape the city's climate responses. Chapter 6 discusses in more depth Boston's recent actions, risks, and opportunities related to climate change mitigation and adaptation. In conclusion, Chapter 7 synthesizes these findings by imagining some future scenarios for Boston's next decades.

The city's climate response is highly dynamic. My goal is to provide enough detail to make sense of the landscape of climate risks in Boston, the evolution of climate action in the city, and the key issues at stake in its future. I place these local concerns into a broader literature on urban governance of climate change mitigation, adaptation, and equity to contextualize Boston's example and note opportunities for comparisons with other cities. Boston offers a blueprint for evolving climate governance that other cities can learn from. But it also has unique risks and opportunities firmly embedded within historically conditioned systems that shape the adaptive capacities of urban areas and social responses to changing conditions (Wise et al. 2014). Ultimately, a case study like this is useful not simply as a recipe for action but as an argument for basing climate governance on a more nuanced study of urban systems.

What is "Boston"?

Any study of urban climate change governance must reckon with the question: what is the correct unit of scale to examine? Does it make sense talk about "cities" and climate action, when most cities are embedded in sprawling metropolitan areas that are linked by common challenges? Metropolitan growth and political fragmentation play an important a role in Boston's development and urban life. Boston had just under 676,000 residents in the 2020 Census, while Greater Boston is the eleventh largest combined statistical area in the United States, with a population of 4.9 million. While different definitions of the metropolitan area and definitions of fragmentation yield different rankings, Boston is considered "one of the country's most politically fragmented metropolises" (Horan 2009, 349). If you live and work in Boston, you might cross into different cities and towns daily riding the subway or driving down the street, including Cambridge, Somerville, Newton, Brookline, Milton, Quincy, or Chelsea. In Massachusetts, individual municipalities like these have a great deal of control over many of their own decisions and functions, yet they share important infrastructure systems, governance structures, and social and economic continuities. In this book, I focus on the City of Boston itself as the primary unit of interest, since the city has municipal climate strategies distinct from neighboring cities and towns in the metro area, and the city is worth examining in a discussion of urban climate action. But I hope to avoid the traps of "methodological cityism" (Angelo and Wachsmuth 2015), which ignores broader urban entities and processes that shape any particular city. Boston is but a relatively small political and geographical entity in a large and complex metropolis, and it is embedded within larger ecological, social, and infrastructural systems such as resource flows, energy grids, government and regulatory systems, and socioeconomic networks that enable or constrain its ability to act on climate change. From a planning perspective, the larger metropolitan context is also vital to understanding Boston's mitigation and adaptation efforts and challenges, so I refer to metropolitan issues throughout. Advancing climate change mitigation, adaptation, and equity often require working beyond municipal boundaries, so I discuss the role of regional cooperation in Boston's climate action.

Chapter 2

BOSTON'S CLIMATE FOOTPRINT AND RISKS

Occupying just 125.3 square kilometers (48.4 square miles) of land, Boston is the second smallest major U.S. city in area, just behind San Francisco. It has a population of 716,313 (in 2025), which has grown since its nadir of 562,994 in 1980, but is still below its 1950 peak of 801,444. Boston is a relatively densely built city radiating out from a historic port in the innermost shelter of Boston Harbor, an estuary in Massachusetts Bay with three primary tributary rivers (the Charles, Mystic, and Neponset). It occupies a formerly marshy peninsula at the confluence of three primary rivers that has been transformed through centuries of filling tidal and shallow areas adjacent to the coast. Though small for a major city, Boston is embedded within the 11th largest combined metropolitan statistical area in the United States, with a population of nearly 5 million. This geographical region stretches into Manchester, New Hampshire, Cape Cod, Worcester, and Providence, Rhode Island. A narrower but more politically useful definition of Greater Boston might be the 101 cities and towns served by the Metropolitan Area Planning Council (MAPC), or the 21 "inner core" communities that lie between the coast and the I-95 highway with a population of 1.6 million. Boston also lies within the heavily urbanized "megalopolis" or Northeast Megaregion running along the East Coast from Boston to Washington, DC.

Planning for climate change requires cities to orient their governance toward the future in ways that they did not in the past. Robust climate governance at a local scale requires collecting data about the state of the system, projections of climate change impacts, and metrics for evaluating the city's progress along climate-related goals. The City of Boston has established mechanisms for measuring and accounting for its own greenhouse gas emissions and has released an annual citywide emissions inventory since 2005. Its latest annual inventory, from 2023, estimates that the city emits 5.70 million metric tons of greenhouse gasses (GHGs) annually (City of Boston 2024). A comparison of emissions inventories of C40 cities places Boston 11th among 16 North American cities (using its 2019 inventory) (Ahn et al. 2023). A 2018 global comparison of metropolitan carbon footprints ranks the Greater Boston urban area 12th highest in the United States.

By its own accounting (Figure 2.1), about 68% of the city's emissions come from its buildings, with most of the remaining emissions from transportation, and a negligible amount from waste. The city has reduced its emissions by 22% from 2005 levels despite an increase in population. Per person, Boston residents emit an estimated 8 metric tons in 2022 versus 15 metric tons in

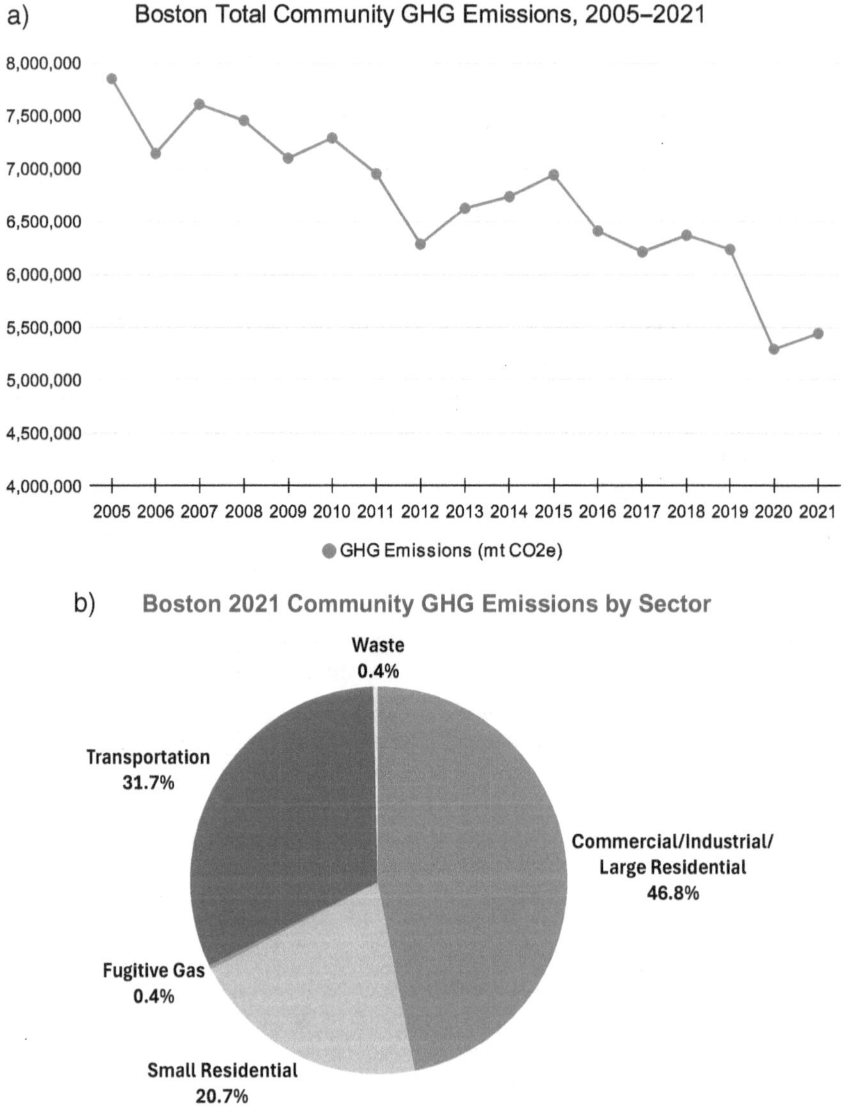

Figure 2.1 (a) Boston's Community Greenhouse Gas Emissions, 2005–2021. Source: City of Boston data. (b) Boston's Community Greenhouse Gas Emission by Sector, 2021. Source: City of Boston data.

2005, a decrease of 42%. Despite this significant recent progress, Boston's overall emissions rose between 2020 and 2022, which the city attributes to higher natural gas use in large buildings (City of Boston 2024). An analysis of Boston's progress in achieving its net-zero goals found that the city is making significant progress but will miss its interim 50% by 2030 target by a few years (Fitzgerald et al. 2022). A significant proportion of Boston's emissions reductions stems from broader forces outside the city's control, including a cleaner electricity grid (replacing coal and oil with energy from natural gas), a decline in the use of fuel oil for heating, and better fuel efficiency in vehicles (City of Boston 2014). Becoming a carbon neutral city will ultimately require moving away from natural gas and other fossil fuels. While this continued transition will also be hastened by market forces and policies at higher levels of government, city municipal government may also need to take more direct and politically difficult steps to phase out fossil fuels in the city.

While Boston's government has pledged to consider creating an emissions inventory that includes consumption of goods and services bought, sold, and used within Boston (City of Boston, 2021), it has never created a consumption-based emissions inventory. The city has many initiatives that encourage reuse and recycling through its Zero Waste plan, but those initiatives are not explicitly designed to reduce consumption-based emissions.

Climate science and modeling have increasingly provided a clearer picture of Boston's future in a changing climate. Policymakers have a growing understanding of which areas of the city will likely experience stormwater flooding, how different areas of the city generate heat islands, and which neighborhoods and infrastructures will be subject to floods during high tides and major storms with sea-level rise. As climate impacts become more visible, projections that once seemed distant in time or space are now becoming more immediate. Bostonians now experience more frequent heat waves and can see regular flooding of areas of the city's waterfront with periodic "king tides." This growing awareness and more precise scientific modeling have helped to shape municipal planning and policy.

Boston has benefitted from downscaled local climate projections for the city and the Boston metro region, as well as a statewide climate change assessment, which together have helped to advance climate preparedness initiatives and policies in the city and region. City-level projections have been made possible by partnerships between city government, private foundations, and scientific and technical experts from local universities and private companies. The Boston Research Advisory Group (BRAG) was created through the city's Climate Ready Boston planning process and issued a 2016 scientific consensus report on the climate impacts expected throughout the century (Douglas et al. 2016). Its findings have been incorporated into city planning and communications about climate change. The BRAG report advocated updating projections every two years; in practice, however, it took six years before an updated scientific consensus report was released in 2022. By that time, many municipalities in the Boston metro area began using information from Climate Ready Boston in their own planning (Valdez 2020), prompting a need to widen the lens of climate science beyond the city's borders. The group was renamed the Greater Boston Research Advisory Group (GBRAG), and a new report was issued after a community engagement process to understand the needs and concerns of other communities in the metropolitan area, as well as to consider the impacts of climate change on the region's environmental justice communities (Valdez 2020). Much of the information below derives from two reports, as well as from metropolitan climate change analyses from MAPC and the state of Massachusetts' Climate Change Assessment, which evaluates climate hazards in the state and ranks impacts based on urgency across various sectors and by region, including in the metropolitan core around Boston Harbor (Commonwealth of Massachusetts 2022b).

Temperature Changes

Although global temperature increases with greenhouse gas emissions are well understood, making projections at local scales involves greater uncertainty and a widening range of likely future temperatures at longer time frames. Short-term warming over the next decade or two is relatively locked in as a function of past and current greenhouse gas emissions but warming later in the century will depend largely on actions taken globally to curb emissions. UCCRN ARC3.2 temperature projections for Boston include a temperature increase of 1.2–3°C by the 2050s, and 1.5–4.9°C by the 2080s (Rosenzweig et al. 2018). Local projections include a rise in average maximum temperatures of 2.8–5.2°C by the 2080s to 2100s in Boston (Douglas and Kirshen 2022).

Among cities in the United States, Boston has the benefit of a relatively northern latitude (42.33°) compared to most major US cities. But extreme heat, defined here as days reaching over 90° in the summer, has been a growing part of Boston's summers, accounting for about 10 days per year in 2000 and projected to occur 16–26 days yearly by 2030 and 21–80 days yearly by 2080 (Douglas and Kirshen 2022). Heat waves in Boston are frequently accompanied by high humidity, which contributes significantly to heat stress and is a health concern with climate change (Coffel et al. 2017), although measures that incorporate both temperature and humidity, such as wet bulb globe temperature, have not been incorporated into official city or state policy. The Massachusetts Climate Change Assessment identifies health impacts from extreme heat as the most urgent impact in the Boston Harbor region, which includes much of the densely populated metro area, given that it already sees more temperature-related premature deaths than the state average (Commonwealth of Massachusetts 2022b). Rising temperatures are expected to worsen air quality in the metropolitan area. Extreme heat, increased droughts, and changes in pests may threaten urban tree cover in the metropolitan area, making it challenging to improve and expand the urban forest (Commonwealth of Massachusetts 2022b). Demand for heating in the winter is expected to decrease over time, but higher summer temperatures will put greater demand on the electricity grid through greater use of air conditioning (Douglas and Kirshen 2022). Periods of extreme heat could also potentially damage roads, rail lines, and other infrastructure.

Boston's built environment creates a heterogenous experience for its residents during heat waves. There are wide disparities in outdoor temperatures of different neighborhoods during periods of extreme heat based on urban density and design, as well as disparities in thermal comfort based on building type and access to air conditioning. These differences raise challenges for adaptation and environmental justice that will be explored in the following sections.

Boston's natural ecosystems have already been impacted by climate change; in particular, New England coastal waters have warmed more than any other in the United States, impacting local cod and lobster fisheries. Continued ocean warming in combination with ocean acidification could threaten local fish and shellfish industries that are important to the Boston region (Commonwealth of Massachusetts 2022b). Extended droughts in summer have also been impacting natural ecosystems. Warmer winters in the Boston area are expected to lengthen the growing season, which will likely benefit some forms of local agriculture but threaten some traditional products that depend on cold winters, such as cranberries and maple syrup (Douglas and Kirshen 2022). The region has seen growing incidences of Lyme disease and other tick-borne illnesses.

Precipitation

Boston receives more than 43 inches of precipitation each year. Climate change has already increased annual precipitation by 70% in the Northeast between 1958 and 2010, particularly in warmer months, largely because of more intense rainstorms (Douglas and Kirshen 2022). In the future, this trend is expected to continue and may include increased precipitation in the winter and spring. The most intense rainstorms today are heavier than they were in the previous century, and extreme precipitation events are projected to increase by up to 40% over this century (Metropolitan Area Planning Council 2023), causing larger and more frequent river floods and greater stormwater flooding. Stormwater runoff is already a major source of pollution to waterways in the Boston area, and a growing intensity of rain events could exacerbate impacts to water quality, as well as freshwater and marine ecosystems (Commonwealth of Massachusetts 2022b). Rising groundwater levels in parts of the metro areas could contribute to flooding risks (Douglas and Kirshen 2022). An MAPC-led analysis of heavy rainstorms in 2010 suggests that current federal flood maps do not capture the full extent of inland flood-prone areas (Metropolitan Area Planning Council 2023).

Sea-Level Rise and Storm Surge

Relative sea levels in Boston Harbor have risen faster than the global average, and the pace of change is accelerating. From 2001 to 2019, they rose an average of 5.4 mm per year, about twice as fast as the previous century's average (Douglas and Kirshen 2022). As is true globally, projections for sea-level rise in Boston are well understood over the next couple of decades but vary widely later in the century depending on the emissions scenario, underscoring how the city's long-term fate rests on widespread actions to curb global greenhouse gas emissions. With greatly reduced emissions, sea-level rise could remain under 30 inches by 2100, while a high-emission future could result in 6.5 feet of sea-level rise by that time. Historically, global sea-level rise has largely been accounted for by thermal expansion of the oceans due to rising temperatures, but recently the melting of ice sheets in Greenland and Antarctica has become the primary contributor. Due to gravitational forces, ice loss from the West Antarctic Ice Sheet will have a particularly grave impact on sea-level rise in Boston (25% higher than the global average) (Douglas and Kirshen 2022). Massive losses of ice from this ice sheet would result in catastrophic flooding in coastal areas in and around Boston beyond these projections.

Boston Harbor is buffered from powerful Atlantic storms by the land forming the outer arms of the Harbor—particularly Hull to the South and Winthrop to the North—and a series of Harbor Islands that were once a field of glacial drumlins scattered across the basin. This geography has helped to diminish the impact of coastal hurricanes and storms in Boston and other communities within Boston Harbor. Even so, the coastal cities and towns of Metro Boston together contain about 11,000 hectares of land (10% of the total land area) within a 100-year storm floodplain (Kirshen et al. 2008). Rising sea levels will expand this floodplain and make current design storm flooding levels more frequent. In Boston, a storm surge that has a 1% annual chance of occurring (a 100-year flood) could have a 20% chance of occurring by the 2050s (Douglas et al. 2016). Rising seas would gradually deepen Boston

Harbor, diminish the cumulative landmass of the islands, and eventually overwhelm many salt marshes and other natural coastal ecosystems, particularly given the density of development that allows little room for marsh migration (Douglas et al. 2016).

Boston is hit by relatively few tropical cyclones (hurricanes), but the growing intensity of hurricanes that is widely projected to occur with climate change could result in greater impacts from those that do reach the city, while the more common nor'easters, which can hover over the same area for a day or more, have a greater likelihood of producing coastal flooding, particularly when the storm coincides with high tides (Douglas et al. 2016). Because Boston has a relatively high tidal range of nearly 10 feet, tidal cycles have an important influence on the likelihood of coastal flood events. The confluence of storm intensity, tidal cycles, and sea-level rise will shape coastal flood hazards in Boston, particularly in large waterfront areas situated on low-lying filled lands. A rise in sea levels of 1.5 feet over 2000 levels could expose more than 10% of the built environment to storm flooding and about 5% to regular tidal flooding (City of Boston 2016).

Boston has benefited from detailed projections of future flooding with sea-level rise, which provide block-by-block projections of flooding frequencies and depths in high-risk areas. A hydrodynamic model developed in 2015 as part of a study for the Massachusetts Department of Transportation projects storm floods with sea-level rise (Bosma et al. 2015), and has been incorporated into city planning. While coastal areas in Boston and its metropolitan area are vulnerable to flooding, even inland neighborhoods and towns such as Allston, Cambridge, Arlington, Somerville, and Everett could be flooded by storms toward the end of the century, because they are protected by two critical dams, the New Charles River Dam and the Amelia Earhart Dam on the lower Mystic River, which block tidal flows into the city's major rivers (Douglas and Kirshen 2022). Composite floods consisting of both heavy precipitation and storm surge could also pose challenges in the future, although a GBRAG analysis finds a relatively low risk of co-occurrence of extreme rainfall and extreme storm surge (Douglas and Kirshen 2022).

Cumulative and Synergistic Impacts

The projected changes in weather patterns this century, summarized in Figure 2.2, can have cumulative or synergistic impacts on Boston's infrastructure systems, public health, and the urban economy. Climate change will make it more challenging for Bostonians to rely on functioning emergency response systems, transportation networks, food supply chains, and energy grids (Commonwealth of Massachusetts 2022b). Boston could

	Annual Precipitation (inches)		Design floods (100-year)	Average Daily Max Temp (°F)		Average Daily Min Temp (°F)	
Baseline	46.07 (1971–2000)			59.7 (1990–2010)		39.5 (1990–2010)	
2050s	RCP 4.5	+0.7 to +5.4	−10% to +35%	RCP 4.5	+3.6	RCP 4.5	+4.0
	RCP 8.5	+0.4 to +6.7		RCP 8.5	+4.5	RCP 8.5	+5.0
2090s	RCP 4.5	+1.7 to +5.9	+15% to +70%	RCP 4.5	+5.0	RCP 4.5	+5.5
	RCP 8.5	+0.7 to +9.5		RCP 8.5	+9.1	RCP 8.5	+9.8

Figure 2.2 Projected changes in annual precipitation, major storms, and average daily temperatures in the Boston area. Data source: Douglas and Kirshen (2022).

see escalating impacts on transportation networks, including the effect of delays and lost trips due to riverine and coastal flooding (Suarez et al. 2005), such as along the flood-prone Blue Line subway that serves East Boston and neighboring cities. Long-term climate stressors may also degrade aspects of Boston's quality of life, including air and water quality, emotional and cognitive health, recreational and cultural resources, and economic stability (Commonwealth of Massachusetts 2022b). Air pollution, largely driven by fine particulate matter emitted from fossil fuel combustion, is a significant public health problem and an environmental justice issue in the Boston area. High particulate levels combined with longer pollen seasons with climate change could exacerbate asthma and other respiratory problems that have a higher burden in environmental justice communities. By the same token, achieving decarbonization across the city would confer health benefits to residents, particularly impacting communities of color (Raifman et al. 2020). These connections between climate hazards and risks highlight the importance of taking action on climate change in a way that integrates climate mitigation measures and climate adaptation and disaster risk reduction (Rosenzweig et al. 2018).

Chapter 3

BOSTON'S ADAPTIVE CAPACITIES IN HISTORICAL CONTEXT

Boston's climate risks and ability to mitigate and adapt to climate change are shaped by the 400-year environmental, social, economic, and infrastructural history of the city's development. Urban development brings profound physical changes to natural environments. It has a complex history of socioeconomic and racial inequality that shapes the vulnerabilities and risks of its neighborhoods. And it has a history of economic prosperity, decline, and reinvention that shapes its social and financial systems. Boston's ability to mitigate and adapt to climate change is highly influenced by this social, ecological, and infrastructural past. Many of the climate-related decisions facing the city and greater metropolitan area today involve updating the city's aging stormwater, natural gas, and transportation infrastructure for a changing climate. Past decisions have also given the city advantages, including a robust water and sewage system and a public transit network that makes the tasks of mitigation and adapting to climate change much more achievable. Rather than attempting to recount Boston's storied history in detail, this chapter considers aspects of its environmental, infrastructural, and social history that are particularly salient for considering its climate risks and opportunities.

Urban infrastructural systems are interconnected with natural ecological systems and socio-economic systems (Pandit et al. 2017). Built infrastructure is a long-lived technological intervention, so infrastructural decisions in urban areas often create path-dependent relationships that lock in specific adaptation pathways (Tellman et al. 2018) or create recurring patterns that persist within the SETS over time (Markolf et al. 2018). In the SETS framework (see Figure 3.1), technological intervention often mediates relationships within ecological and social systems. Infrastructural systems are highly path dependent, though they do change as they are repaired, updated, expanded, and reconfigured (Moss 2020). The way that infrastructure is governed can aid or hinder the goal of urban transformation toward greater sustainability (Monstadt et al. 2022). While most SETS research has been concerned with

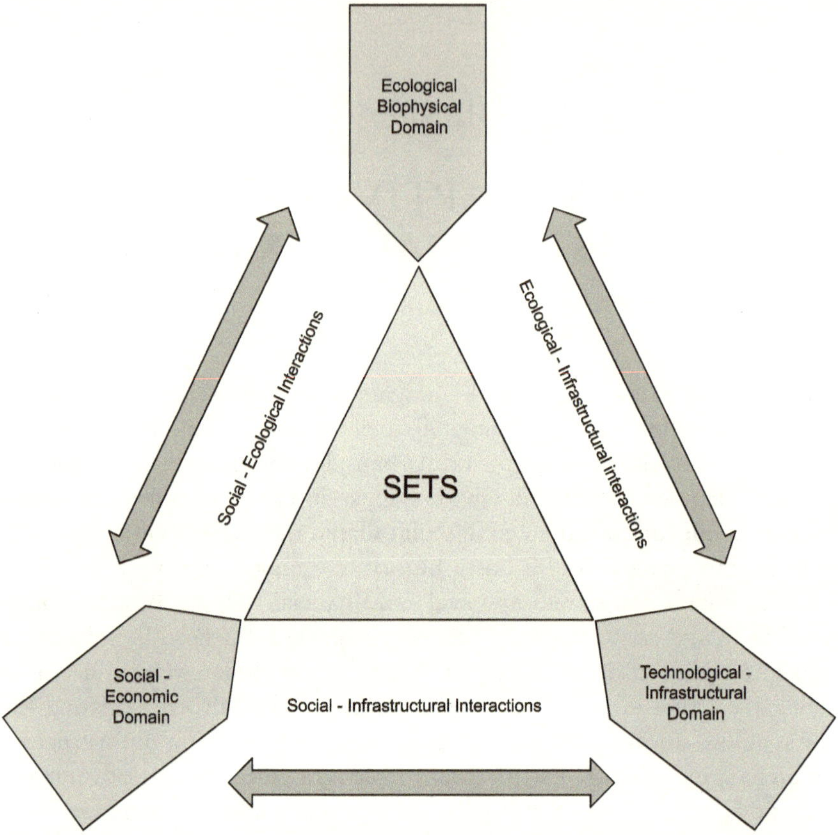

Figure 3.1 The social-ecological-technological systems (SETS) conceptual framework for understanding urban dynamics. Adapted from (McPhearson et al. 2022).

contemporary cities and their current management, the SETS framework also lends itself to historical analysis of urban systems, which is critical for understanding how urban areas evolve and how interactions between social, ecological, and technological dimensions of a system unfold over time. For this reason, history is not mere background but an essential part of describing and understanding how governance and decision-making have shaped the system and its adaptation pathways (Tellman et al. 2018).

It can be challenging to disentangle the social, ecological, and technological dimensions of complex systems as they are highly intertwined and often overlap. Here, I trace distinct adaptation pathways within Boston's history that highlight different facets of SETS interactions and their impact on climate change mitigation and adaptation: land expansion, land use and transportation, sanitary infrastructure development, urban development and social inequality, metropolitan expansion, and economic growth. These brief histories are intended to both paint a portrait of Boston and to offer a way of linking urban histories to contemporary urban policy debates around climate change by detailing the unfolding of the SETS within which urban climate change governance acts. This background will set the stage for exploring Boston's governance systems and specific opportunities and challenges in responding to climate challenges.

Land Expansion and Coastal Change

Boston's urban development shares features with other North American port cities that emerged as central shipping and trade centers within harbors. But the city is also unique in the scale of the physical transformation of its harbor over time, particularly the tremendous expansion of land beyond its natural footprint at the expense of wetland ecosystems. The city has more made land than any other in North America; it added 5,250 acres of new land throughout its history, amounting to one-sixth of the current land area (Seasholes 2018). Almost all the city's original salt marshes have disappeared, as have numerous freshwater wetlands, while urban development constricted its three major rivers (the Charles, Mystic, and Neponset) and buried some of the city's smaller waterways. In the SETS framework, Boston's made land and altered wetlands constitute an ecological transformation driven by social and economic change that have systemwide impacts with consequences for the city's climate risks.

Boston's natural environment is shaped by glacial activity that left a watery landscape after the last glacial maximum around 13,000 years ago. As sea levels gradually stabilized, populations of hunter-gatherers coalesced around the rivers and estuary that fed into Boston Harbor, including tidal areas of the Charles River and the bay behind the Shawmut peninsula (Bagley 2007). Boston's wetlands and sheltered harbor shaped social-ecological relationships in the area before colonial settlement and urbanization. Algonquian groups in the region, including the Massachusett, the Narragansett, and the Wampanoag, based territorial power on social relationships and kin networks, and they typically asserted the right of the community to use hunting, gathering, or farming grounds as part of a collective homeland (Brooks 2018). Different groups defined territories based on river drainages and adopted a pattern of seasonal mobility within estuarial spaces as a response to changing conditions in the availability and distribution of resources throughout the year (Patton 2014).

Ecological conditions thus drove a flexibly mobile way of life well suited to the changeable and dynamic conditions of New England ecosystems, including the shoreline. *Mashauwomuk*, the Massachusetts name for the peninsula that became Boston, meant "the place to land mishoons," a reference to the canoes commonly used by Native people to traverse coastal waters—a commentary on its position as a watery access point to other sites in the harbor (Massachusett Tribe, n.d.). This name also reflects how indigenous peoples regard dynamic coastal areas like this peninsula as critical sites for travel, resource collection, social interaction, and temporary occupation—but not sites of fixed settlement or cultivation.

European colonial settlement profoundly altered these dynamics. When Puritans originally founded Boston in 1630, it was surrounded by extensive marshes and mudflats and joined to the mainland only by a narrow bridge of land. This preexisting ecology, combined with a social and economic need to connect the newfound settlements to colonial trade networks, led to immediate reconfiguration of the natural environment through waterfront infrastructure. To aid this transformation, the colonial government encouraged private landowners to construct wharves and docks, beginning the process of hardening the shoreline. New land was initially created by filling between and around previously built infrastructure, such as wharves and a mill pond, but eventually included projects to fill mudflats adjacent to land.

By the nineteenth century, public and private actors increasingly created new land along the waterfront for a variety of uses, including railroad infrastructure, industrial facilities, residential neighborhoods, and new parkland. As described extensively by historian Nancy Seasholes, Boston's land-making efforts were often driven by private real estate ventures, public civic and infrastructure projects, and population growth.

Land-making was also a response to ecological degradation driven by previous infrastructure encroachments, a type of infrastructural fix to the evolving social and ecological conditions of the urban SETS. For instance, the filling of Back Bay, one of Boston's central neighborhoods, was justified both by a desire to retain elite residents in a city overwhelmed by an influx of immigrants and by poor environmental conditions created by sewage in the tidal river and drainage obstructed by tidal dams and railroads. In the early twentieth century, the mouth of the Charles River was finally dammed, transforming the problematic tidal estuary into a freshwater park flanked by roads, green spaces, and public walkways (Haglund 2003). By this time, areas that were once lapped by tidal waters, like the edge of the city's iconic Boston Common, were now inland and many of the city's densest neighborhoods rested on fill. The last large-scale fill project in Boston was filling of the East Boston Flats to create and expand Logan Airport in the twentieth century, which swallowed up five small islands and created a sprawling 2000 acres of land (Seasholes 2018).

Boston's made land has been central to its continued economic growth, as many of the neighborhoods once filled for industrial and commercial purposes have been redeveloped into mixed-use neighborhoods and office and lab space. But widespread land-making has profound ecological consequences. Boston's made land, depicted against the original shoreline in Figure 3.2(a), overlaps considerably with the city's projected flood plain

a)

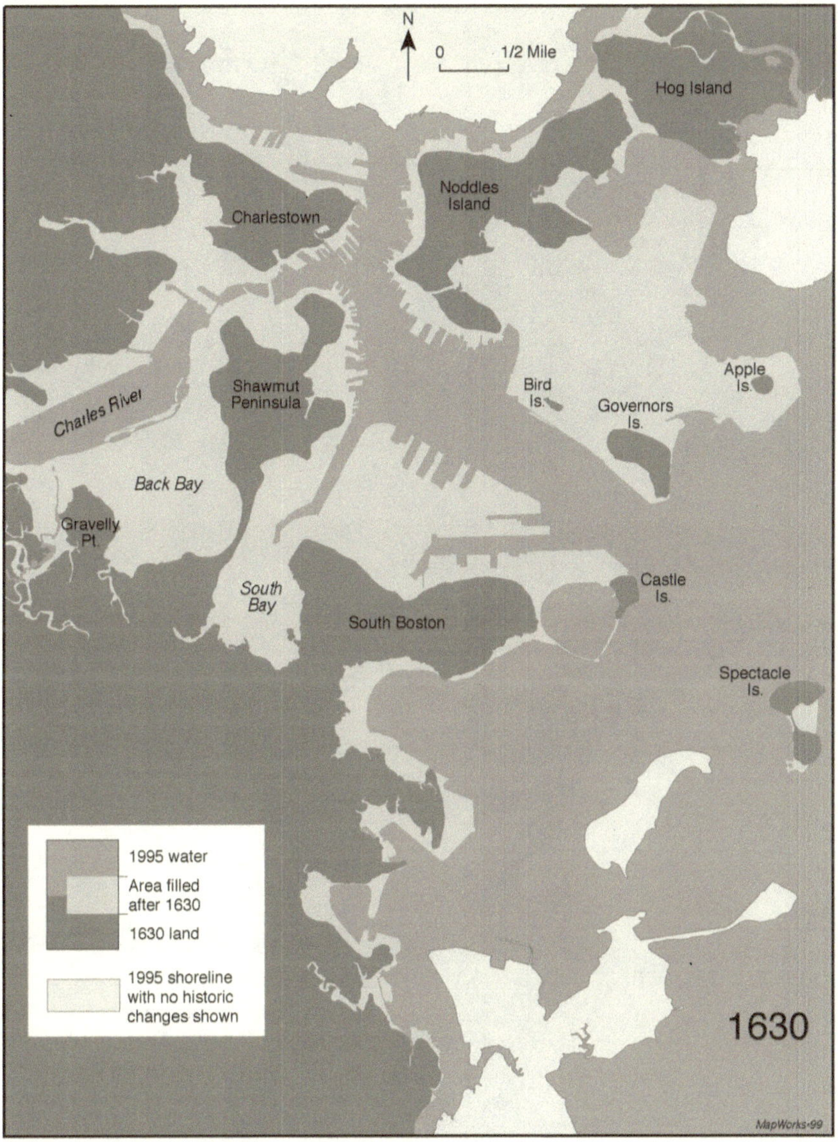

Figure 3.2 (a) Boston shoreline 1630. Map Works, Inc. Copyright © The Muriel G. and Norman B. Leventhal Family Foundation. (b) Flood progression—coastal and riverine flooding in Boston with 36 inches of sea-level rise. Rendered in QGIS from City of Boston data.

with sea-level rise expected later in the century. Figure 3.2(b) shows expected flooding with 36 inches of sea level rise at monthly high tides and during 10% and 1% annual chance flood events. The city boldly refashioned its own geography by creating low-lying land, but in doing so has left some of

b)

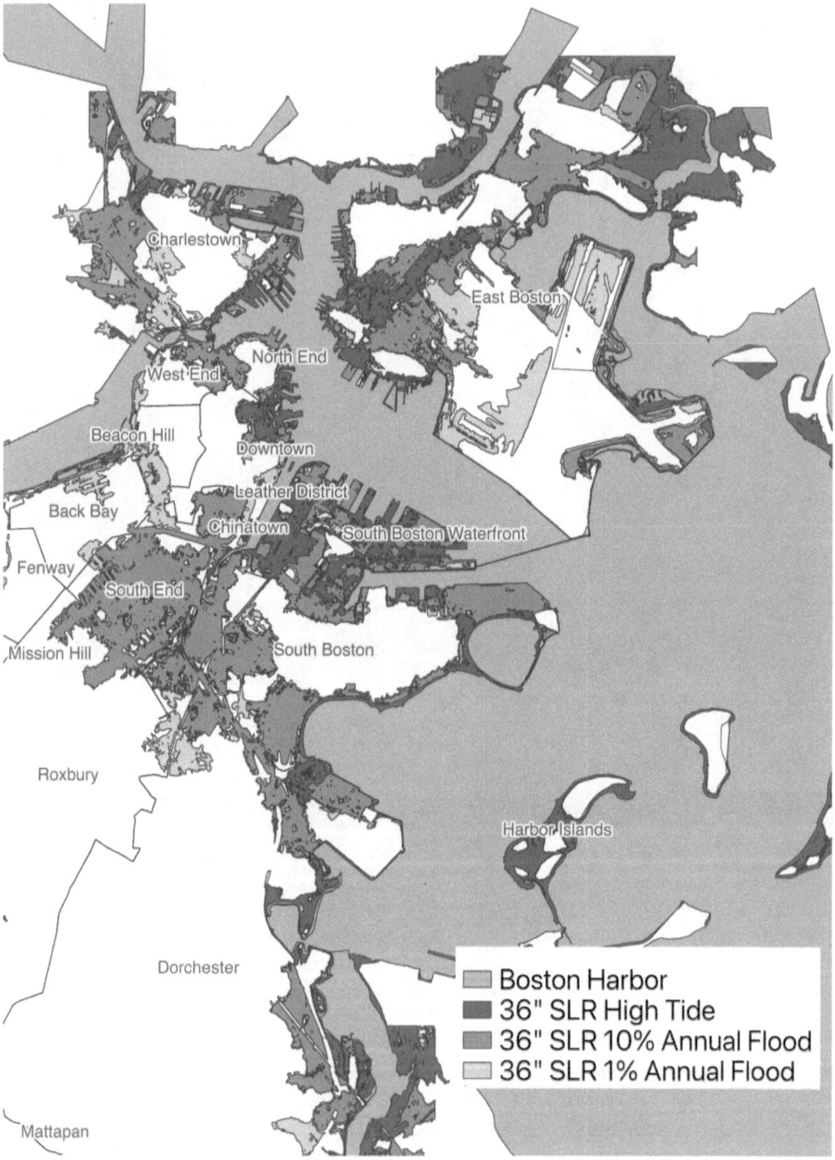

Figure 3.2 *(continued)*

the city's most economically important neighborhoods and infrastructure vulnerable to flooding, including Back Bay, parts of its downtown waterfront, East Boston and Logan Airport, and the recently redeveloped Seaport District. Filled land also brings additional issues with contaminated soils, seismic risk, and land subsidence. The city's Back Bay neighborhood was constructed on wooden piles that could degrade with changing groundwater levels, necessitating ongoing groundwater monitoring.

Bostonians constructed their own future floodplain and have been working to plan to protect it for more than a decade. This specific Boston context shares parallels with the development histories of other North American cities built on large areas of reclaimed land and fill, including Manhattan, San Francisco, Miami, and Toronto. In filling urban wetlands, these cities removed ecologically based flood control systems that dampened waves and buffered developed land from storms. Boston's shoreline development supports longstanding observations that infrastructure hardening builds system robustness at the expense of flexibility, ultimately resulting in greater vulnerability (Carpenter et al. 2015). A hardened shoreline is maximized for socioeconomic purposes at the expense of ecological resilience (Chapman and Underwood 2011; Gittman et al. 2016). About 58% of Boston Harbor's shoreline is protected by some kind of engineered structure (Fontenault et al. 2013), limiting opportunities for wetland restoration and leaving many communities dependent on shoreline structures for their continued protection.

Land Use Patterns, Transportation, and Open Space

The adaptive capacities of cities are shaped by their unique development patterns, including urban density, sprawl, road and transportation networks, and the availability of parks and intact natural ecosystems. Boston's development history highlights ongoing interactions between development, transportation infrastructure, and open space. These patterns of development help to shape the city's carbon footprint, its landscapes of risk across the city, and its opportunities to adapt to and mitigate climate change.

Oliver Wendall Holmes once satirically wrote that Bostonians viewed the city's State House as "the hub of the solar system," and Bostonians eagerly adopted the nickname "The Hub" or "The Hub of the Universe" to describe their city. More than just a mindset, the hub is also a useful metaphor to describe Boston's inland physical development, as the growing city radiated outward from its central colonial port and downtown (including Beacon Hill where the State House lies). As Boston added land on its shoreline, it also expanded inland, annexing some of its adjacent towns as it grew from a port town into a city. The original Shawmut peninsula retains its famously convoluted web of colonial streets, while downtown neighborhoods that were filled in the nineteenth century were often laid out with regular grids and boulevards. Boston was an early example of suburbanization as both a land use pattern and a system of socioeconomic separation (Warner 1978). Suburbs originally began in the nineteenth century as village-like centers flanked by single-family homes that served as communities and summer residences for the affluent. Travel to and from these suburbs was made possible first by omnibuses drawn by horses, and later in the century by streetcar lines. So-called streetcar suburbs developed along major thoroughfares radiating from the city center, allowing wealthier residents to move farther from the center while lower-income residents were tied to areas served by crosstown streetcars (Warner 1978).

While the city's commercial Downtown and innermost neighborhoods have a high density, Boston's outer neighborhoods to the south and west—Roxbury, Dorchester, Mattapan, Jamaica Plain, and West Roxbury—are shaped by this early wave of suburbanization. They retain a less urban character, with busy thoroughfares and commercial hubs surrounded by quiet, tree-lined residential side streets. These areas rapidly filled with multifamily buildings in the late nineteenth century, including the hallmark three-deckers that give Boston-area neighborhoods their distinct character, including supporting ethnic enclaves.

As the city grew, Boston's leaders worked to reshape its environment to provide parks and park systems. These systems sometimes helped to preserve natural ecosystems, but they often involved significant transformation of natural systems to manage pollution and create spaces suitable for public recreational use. Boston was the first city to engage landscape architect Frederic Law Olmsted to design an interconnected park system across the city, known as the Emerald Necklace, which incorporated drainage management into public parkland. Throughout the nineteenth century, the city engaged in numerous efforts to reshape the Charles River as a public space, including damming the river and creating a waterfront park called the Esplanade that created a controlled environment removed from tidal changes (Haglund 2003). At the end of the nineteenth century, city leaders created a Metropolitan Park System that preserved "reservations" of open space in Greater Boston that helped to shape future suburban development patterns and modulate urban density and private land uses (Moga 2009). Nineteenth century park systems had explicitly social aims, including improving public health and sanitation and providing democratic urban spaces. They were not designed as islands of green space but as interconnected spaces for multimodal transportation systems (O'Connell 2016). But they paradoxically laid the groundwork for the region's outward spread; parkways built to give people access to the reservations became corridors of development and regional highways in the automobile age (O'Connell 2013).

With its radial density pattern, Boston offers an example of the tradeoffs between density and open space in urban life, climate change mitigation, and adaptation. Its relatively dense character around its central urban "hub" limits urban greenhouse gas emissions generated by sprawl, and its well-established public transportation system, which includes the subway, bus, and commuter rail systems, provides viable low-emission public transportation to many people in and around the city. Boston's land use development also has significant consequences for climate change impacts and adaptation across the city. Temperature maps of heat in Boston (see Figure 3.3) show a highly variable landscape that reflects its outward expansion: areas that resist the most extreme temperatures in a heat wave are largely found in and around extensive green spaces in the southwest neighborhoods like Franklin Park and Stony Brook Reservation and in lower-density neighborhoods with high tree canopy cover. In contrast, much of the downtown core can reach temperatures over 100°F during heat waves, and these denser areas tend to remain extremely hot overnight (City of Boston 2022b).

Boston's public transportation system is still marked by a hub-and-spoke design in which subway and rail facilitate suburb-to-downtown commutes, while buses often provide the only crosstown connections. The city's early public transit systems were largely privately owned and decentralized, until a city transit commission was formed to oversee the public financing and construction of the nation's first subway tunnel in 1897 to alleviate

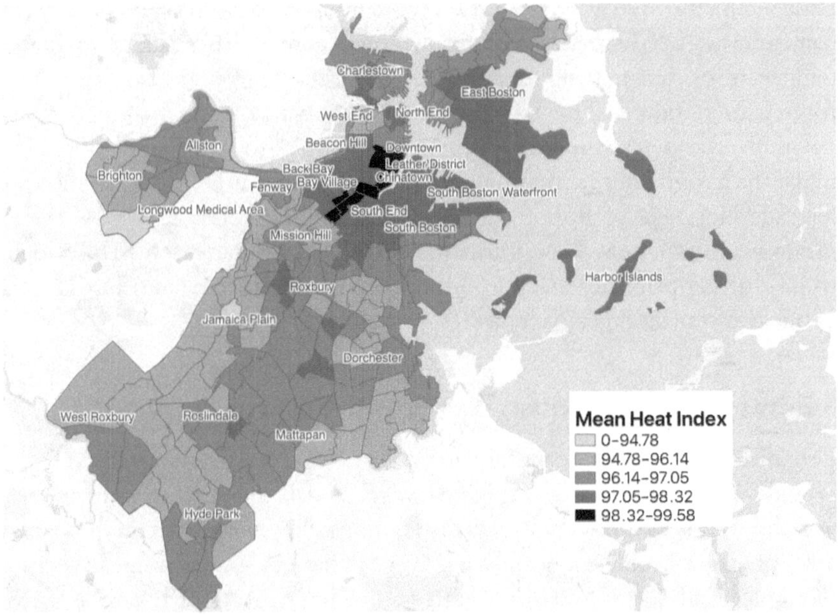

Figure 3.3 Mean summer heat index measured in degrees Fahrenheit for three 1-hour periods in July 2019. Rendered in QGIS from City of Boston data.

downtown traffic. Several elevated streetcar and subway lines were then constructed in the first half of the twentieth century, gradually replacing streetcar lines. New highway construction in and around Boston helped to facilitate suburban growth and a decline in Boston's population and economic output. A poorly planned Central Artery project brought a highway through downtown, cutting off areas of the city without ameliorating traffic congestion as hoped. The state of Massachusetts created a public Metropolitan Transit Authority in 1947, which was later expanded to the Massachusetts Bay Transportation Authority (MBTA) in 1964. The MBTA took control of suburban commuter rail lines and bus routes, while rationalizing the subway system.

In the late twentieth century, Boston embarked on one of the most complex and expensive public infrastructure projects of the modern era with the Central Artery Tunnel or "Big Dig," which put the ill-conceived Central Artery underground. The Big Dig was more than a tunnel, as it involved a complex web of bridges, roads, tunnels, and highway connections, and it was tied to new public transportation, including the MBTA's Silver Line. It created new open spaces, freeing up 30 acres of open space in the Downtown core, now called the Rose Kennedy Greenway. Boston's Big Dig illustrates how investments in public transportation and parkland have complex effects on local economies, social structures, and the physical environment. The Rose Kennedy Greenway, for instance, created new parkland and pedestrian connections that help make the downtown core more resilient to hotter temperatures, but putting a critical highway underground also exposes its tunnels to flooding. The Big Dig's new open space contributed to rising downtown property values that support economic growth (Tajima 2003) but make the urban core increasingly unaffordable, and it helped pave the way for redevelopment of Boston's Seaport District, now one of its most flood-prone neighborhoods. New infrastructure spending increased MBTA debt while shifting priorities away from ongoing maintenance, contributing to a public transportation crisis today (Horan 2025).

Sanitary Infrastructure, Water, and Governance

Urbanization involves reconfiguring natural water systems and cycles to provide drinking water and expel sewage, and it alters freshwater bodies, wetlands, and coastal habitats. Cities' relationship with water is an important aspect of their evolution, both as a driver of changes in urban infrastructure (Kaushal et al. 2015) and as a nexus within urban systems that is sensitive to other social, ecological, and infrastructural developments. As the climate changes, these historical and ongoing actions bring acute problems to cities and metropolitan regions, as they face vulnerabilities and risks that are directly related to past decision making around urban development and water infrastructure.

Boston has followed a classic Global North trajectory of urban evolution around water management, from an industrial city struggling with overcrowding and pollution, to a model "sanitary city" (Melosi 2000) that developed publicly funded infrastructure and expansive government management systems, to a sustainable city working toward improving environmental protections, resource efficiency, recycling, and reduced consumption (Childers et al. 2014; Kaushal et al. 2015). In the nineteenth century, Boston was a leader in developing public water and sewer infrastructure to improve public health and safety. In doing so, it altered the natural watershed hydrology of Eastern Massachusetts while forging a more active role for government in regulating urban life. Managing its waste and pollution, however, has been an ongoing problem. Today, Boston faces challenges shared by numerous cities in maintaining and updating its infrastructure in a changing climate. But the repeated cycles of managing ongoing urban environmental problems also created governance systems that give the city an advantage in responding to climate challenges.

Viewing Boston's evolving water and sewer systems as embedded within a metropolitan SETS underscores how infrastructure is often developed in response to social-ecological problems. The city constructed its first municipal water system in 1848 after facing widespread cholera outbreaks and growing problems addressing urban fires in its built environment. After debates about the best source of water, city leaders chose to bring it from a reservoir constructed west of the city at higher ground via aqueduct (Rawson, 2010). This decision locked in an adaptive pathway in which the city and its growing metropolitan area would look increasingly farther west for its water supply, eventually creating a reservoir 60 miles west of the city in the twentieth century. Like New York City, Boston has the advantage of creating water infrastructure that relies on distant, protected ecosystems; the water system now provides abundant and high-quality water supply to 2.5 million people in the metro area. It has led to ongoing tensions between the metropolitan core and the exurban and rural communities surrounding it over water supply and recreational access to protected reservoirs (Steinberg and Clark 1999).

Managing the city's wastes has been more challenging. The nineteenth-century municipal water system created immediate new burdens for the city's system of sewers, which was designed to funnel rainwater and wastewater, and the rise of flushing water closets created unanticipated new demand for water (Seasholes 2018). Boston chose a solution that would collect sewage and carry it further out to deeper water in Boston Harbor, essentially solving the problem of pollution through dilution (Rudnick 2009). The construction of a comprehensive sewerage system began in 1877 and continued to 1884, and city leaders chose to follow Chicago's example by creating a combined sewer system for stormwater and waste, a consequential decision that created costly path dependencies that the city is still dealing with today. Creating new sanitary infrastructure led to a more expansive perspective on the role of municipal government in providing services to its residents (Rawson, 2010). Access to city services was a major reason that Boston began to grow as it annexed nearby cities and towns, but as the water and sewer systems expanded and gained metropolitan governance systems. In contrast to these large government-led projects, gas and electricity were supplied by private utilities, but often financed with taxes and coordinated by the city (Kennedy 1992), setting up a longstanding adaptive pathway in which water and sewer issues are addressed through public financing.

While Boston's sewerage infrastructure was gradually updated, state leaders largely ignored public complaints of poor water quality and persisted in dumping sludge and raw sewage into the Harbor (Rudnick 2009). The problem languished until the 1980s, when Boston Harbor was infamously dubbed the "Harbor of shame" by George H. W. Bush during his presidential campaign. A local lawsuit eventually led to the creation of a new agency, the Massachusetts Water Resources Authority, to oversee both water and sewerage resources. A federal court order launched an expensive but highly effective clean-up effort, which has transformed the natural environment of the Harbor in recent decades. The primary transformation came from new infrastructure: a state-of-the-art secondary sewage treatment plant (the Deer Island Treatment Plant) and a long-term effort to close or reroute many of the combined sewer overflows that pour sewage into the harbor during heavy precipitation events. This has improved water quality and robust aquatic ecosystems in the Harbor; Boston's beaches are largely safe for swimming. Cleaner water and a more attractive harbor have helped to fuel the waterfront real estate boom while bringing more attention and investment to improving the Boston Harbor Islands and other public spaces near the water (Jin et al. 2018).

The Boston Harbor Clean-Up, like the Big Dig, exemplifies Boston's recent success overcoming path dependencies in its infrastructural systems, but at great public cost. The clean-up effort, however, has been more than an infrastructural quick fix. While built infrastructure helped to solve Boston's sewage crisis, new social-ecological relationships forged through the Boston Harbor Clean-Up have also advanced ecological stewardship through institutional formation and collaboration, including a robust network of government, non-profit, and community groups working toward environmental protection, restoration, and public access (Rudnick 2009).

Managing urban challenges such as water and waste require dynamic governance capacities, which are also important for addressing climate change (Koop et al. 2017). Boston's sanitary journey highlights the cyclical and interconnected nature of social, ecological, and technological relationships and feedbacks within urban systems. It is still incomplete; some area beaches, rivers, and tributaries still receive poor water quality grades. The primary problem is nonpoint source pollution from the dozens of municipalities along its riverfronts and shorelines, which have different capacities to address the problem by implementing stormwater infrastructure and other measures. Continuing to improve water quality is a complex governance problem that has prompted watershed-level stewardship of ongoing pollution issues. Addressing these challenges in a changing climate will require embedding equity, environmental protection, and adaptiveness into decision-making about infrastructure while simultaneously addressing issues of governance scale across municipal boundaries.

Social and Spatial Inequality

In the public imagination, Boston has a reputation of standing for principles of equality and justice throughout its history. The Boston Tea Party is a national symbol of resistance to tyranny. Massachusetts was early in banning slavery and more recently was the first state to allow same-sex marriage. Boston was a center for the abolitionist movement and has nurtured prominent Black leaders and liberal politicians. But Boston's reputation as a leader in progressive politics overlays another history of colonial exploitation, social inequality, ethnic factionalism, and racial struggle. These social inequalities are often spatially expressed through uneven development, investment, and environmental quality. Boston's leaders have made strides in acknowledging and beginning to address these entrenched spatial inequalities, but they remain among the city's major challenges in addressing equity through climate action.

This history begins in Colonial Boston, which includes an under-acknowledged pattern of brutality and land dispossession against Native inhabitants, including one of the most brutal conflicts in Colonial America, King Philip's War, which still leaves deep wounds among Native people in the Boston area today (DeLucia 2018; Young, n.d.). While Massachusetts was the first state to abolish slavery in 1783, enslavement of Native and African people was relatively common in Colonial Boston households. Although New England lacked a major agricultural crop and never formed plantations, Boston's early economic development was tied to slave economies in the West Indies and later to the exploitation of opium smuggling networks to China, both of which had devastating human consequences. In the nineteenth century, Boston became a hub for regional textile manufacturing that depended on cotton from plantations in the South. The visible fruits of these exploitative trade networks were the artistic, cultural, educational, and medical institutions that gave Boston a reputation as a center of learning and progress in the city and region without acknowledging the human and environmental costs.

In the nineteenth century, class and ethnic tensions shaped local politics as Boston's port served as an entry point for waves of immigrants that led to rapid population growth. Tensions between the "Yankee" elite and lower-class white immigrants (particularly the Irish, but also Italians and Eastern Europeans) dominated social dynamics of the Boston region in the nineteenth and early twentieth centuries as Catholic and Jewish immigrants began to change the character of the city. Irish immigrants gradually shifted from forming ethnically limited political and social networks to becoming a dominant force in city and statewide politics (Johnson 2015). Tensions between Irish-Catholic political leaders and the Yankee elite contributed to political and economic stagnation in the twentieth century.

As a center of the abolitionist movement, Boston was a relatively hospitable home for its small population of Black residents in the eighteenth and nineteenth centuries. The post-Civil War era led to an emergence of a Black elite of prominent social members, which historian Adelaide Cromwell calls the "other Brahmins" of Boston (Cromwell 1994). African-American cultural institutions developed in parallel alongside white ones, including cultural and political societies, and some Black civic leaders rose to prominence, including Booker T. Washington, W.E.B. Du Bois, and William Monroe Trotter (Miletsky 2022).

Only 2% of Boston's residents were Black in 1910 (Lundsten et al. 2023), but like many cities in the United States, Boston was transformed by the Great Migration, which brought millions of Black people from the South into cities of the North and West during and after World War II (Gumprecht, 2023). Economic, social, and political opportunities remained limited for Black residents of Boston. Like many cities across the United States, Boston was shaped by discriminatory lending practices for residential mortgages, commonly called redlining. Though most closely associated with the color-coded maps of urban neighborhoods created by the federal Home Owners' Loan Corporation (HOLC) in the late 1930s, which characterized cities spatially according to a scale of desirability and security in lending, redlining also constitutes a more diffuse set of practices across housing agencies and the mortgage lending industry that guided spatially focused discriminatory lending, often along racial lines (Hillier 2003). In Boston, the lowest grades were assigned to communities where Black residents lived, particularly in Roxbury.

While the extent and impacts of redlining practices have been the subject of debate by researchers, there is accumulating evidence that they contributed to long-lived processes of disinvestment, poverty, and low economic mobility in low-graded neighborhoods (Aaronson et al. 2021), as did blockbusting that encouraged white residents to leave diversifying urban communities, and government policies that racially segregated public housing (Gumprecht 2023). Boston saw the racial makeup of neighborhoods like Dorchester and Mattapan change considerably as white residents left for suburban neighborhoods outside the city.

The city's so-called busing crisis in the 1970s has dominated recent histories of social and racial conflict. A federal judicial decision that found that Boston Public Schools had engaged in a "systematic program of segregation" and ordered an immediate and systemwide desegregation of the system, prompting widespread protest in white communities and a long-lasting abandonment of Boston public schools by white families. News coverage at the time emphasized the impact of busing itself, rather than on the history of segregation or the moral impetus to desegregate Boston's schools (Delmont and Theoharis 2017). But scholars have recently revisited this characterization, arguing that busing was merely the most visible conflict in a long history marked by racial tensions between the white and Black populations of the city (Miletsky 2022).

In more recent decades, Boston's population has again been shaped by immigration. In 1970, the foreign-born share of Boston had fallen to 13%, (Delmont and Theoharis 2017), but more than a quarter of Boston's residents are now foreign-born (City of Boston 2017b). Foreign-born residents have driven much of the city's population growth. Today, Boston has robust communities from Haiti, Dominican Republic, China, Brazil, Vietnam, India, and El Salvador, as well as Cape Verde and other African nations, and the Middle East. Some immigrants have settled into lower-income neighborhood enclaves in Boston proper, particularly in Chinatown, East Boston, Mattapan, and Dorchester, but the city has also attracted large numbers of undergraduate and graduate students and professionals from abroad (Johnson 2015).

Beyond its progressive politics, Boston's history provides an uneven set of responses to economic, social, and population changes in relation to principles such as social justice. As a result of this history, the city struggles with deep social divisions that have consequences for how the city and region respond to climate change. Social inequality shapes Boston's ability to engage in just climate action in two important ways.

First, it has led to distributive injustices in exposure to urban risks and access to urban amenities among different communities. Redlining and other discriminatory practices continue to impact infrastructure, green space, and environmental quality in historically underserved neighborhoods (Nardone et al.

2021; Hendricks and Van Zandt 2021). In Boston, racial and class dynamics not only shaped where residents lived but how different neighborhoods developed, which in turn affects their exposure to heat, flooding, and other impacts. Boston's densest neighborhoods (the North End and Chinatown) were developed to house immigrant populations in close quarters. While some of the areas of the dense downtown core are now highly gentrified, Boston also contains heat islands in lower-income neighborhoods. A city-led analysis found that heat waves tend to be hotter and longer in Roxbury, Chinatown, and some other formerly redlined areas of the city (City of Boston 2022b). According to the Trust for Public Land's Park Score, 100% of Bostonians live within a half mile of a park, but people of color and low-income residents have, on average, access to less nearby park space. Areas of Dorchester, Mattapan, and Roxbury, which have high proportions of Black residents, are only serviced by bus (City of Boston 2017b). While coastal flooding impacts wealthier waterfront neighborhoods, it is also a threat for some areas with a high proportion of socially vulnerable residents. East Boston is highly vulnerable to flooding and has a large proportion of residents who are lower-income and foreign-born. In general, Boston's denser inner neighborhoods also tend to have higher proportions of renters who are less able to take steps to improve efficiency and resilience of their housing, and more vulnerable to forces of gentrification.

Second, exclusion based on race, ethnicity, and gender have historically shaped the city's power structures, creating injustices in how different communities participate in climate change transitions and decision-making (procedural injustice) and how their needs and values are recognized in planning (recognition injustice). Boston has officially been a majority non-white city since 2000. Increasingly, racial boundaries have blurred as an increasing number of residents identify as multiracial. Boston has a high degree of income inequality across different racial and ethnic groups. Although the gap has been narrowing, the median annual income of white households in Boston ($134,585 in 2023 according to Census data) is more than twice that of Black households ($59,100) and Hispanic or Latino households ($53,493) and nearly that higher than Asian American ($69,320). Foreign-born residents of Boston have a median income that is less than 60% of native-born residents, and are more likely to live below the poverty line (Granberry et al. 2025). Education is an example of how Boston's broader prosperity is still threatened by serious racial divides in income and wealth. While Boston's elite educational institutions provide a deep pool of expertise and opportunity in sustainability and climate action, the city's public school system has been losing students as affluent and white families leave to suburbs or choose private and charter schools, leaving a system that serves disproportionately students of color and struggles to improve performance in spite of significant per-student investment (Vaznis 2023).

Metropolitan Development

Boston was officially incorporated as a city in 1822. Access to municipal infrastructure was a primary reason that surrounding communities chose to annex to Boston, including Roxbury, Dorchester, and Charlestown (Rawson, 2010). Other communities did not: in 1874, the town of Brookline voted against annexation, a move that demonstrated the growing desire for suburban communities to maintain their character and avoid the problems of the city (O'Connell 2013). Infrastructure became increasingly metropolitan, stretching across multiple cities and towns and governed by special authorities. A push for regional planning led to the creation of a Metropolitan Park System, a system of thousands of acres of reservations and parkways that helped to drive real estate development in suburban communities (O'Connell 2013). Arguments for a broader metropolitan government have surfaced periodically, most prominently in the 1890s, when journalist Sylvester Baxter argued for Boston and its surrounding towns and cities to join into a "federated metropolis" that he called Greater Boston (Merino 1972).

In the twentieth century, most surrounding communities kept their political independence and avoided being absorbed into a city dominated by Irish leaders and a large immigrant population (Kennedy 1992). Boston, meanwhile, became increasingly mired in a political standoff between its Yankee elite and the newly powerful Irish immigrant community. This political stagnation was exacerbated by the trend of deindustrialization and economic losses after World War II. Mid-century suburbanization and "white flight" led to population decline after the city's peak in 1950 (City of Boston 2022a). Not every suburb won out in this dynamic: some industrial-focused suburbs with like Chelsea, Revere, and Lynn experienced a similar downturn as the city (Johnson 2015).

The primary policy response to Boston's economic decline was urban renewal. The Federal Housing Act of 1949 promised federal money for urban renewal projects that would redevelop "blighted" areas of cities. Boston's mayor at that time, John Hynes, sought to create a "New Boston," by building new construction on the ruins of two lower-income, ethnically diverse neighborhoods: the New York Streets in the South End, and the West End (Vrabel 2014). In the 1960s, urban renewal continued under the Boston Redevelopment Authority (BRA), which was given broad powers to both plan the city and direct private development, creating a comprehensive master plan of the city and overseeing the construction of the iconic Prudential Tower, public buildings of Government Center, and numerous civic buildings and housing projects in neighborhoods. On balance, urban renewal helped to stem some of the economic losses of the city and lay the groundwork for a revival, but it also created unanticipated social consequences for the acceptance of government-led planning and redevelopment (Cohen 2020). Urban renewal sparked long-lasting anger and distrust over the city's heavy-handed top-down planning and the destruction of established neighborhoods, a dynamic that challenges neighborhood-level planning today.

Political fragmentation underlies challenges facing the Boston metropolitan region, including in housing, transportation, and economic inequality, and has implications for climate change mitigation and adaptation. Metropolitan authorities still govern water and sewage (now joined together as the Massachusetts Water Resources Authority), and its historical metropolitan parks and roads (now the state Department of Conservation and Recreation). Boston's public transit system is now in crisis, due in part to a failure to secure state-level investments for the ongoing maintenance of the MBTA system. Affluent suburban communities adopted exclusionary zoning laws that contributed to regional sprawl and to an acute housing availability crisis. These zoning policies shifted the burden onto the city to provide affordable and expanded housing options to a growing population. Housing policies have left the metropolitan area with acute spatial segregation and inequality. A recent attempt to seek better balance is the MBTA Communities Act, a state law passed in 2021 requiring 177 cities and towns served by the MBTA to create zoning districts that enable multifamily housing. Boston's fragmentation often leads to a mismatch between political boundaries and ecological resource management, particularly in relation to water. The Charles River, for instance, winds through 35 towns and cities, posing a challenge to efforts to manage stormwater pollution and improve quality in the river.

Social and spatial inequality can be seen across Greater Boston. Industrial facilities and other environmentally hazardous sites are disproportionately concentrated in areas where people of color and lower-income people live (Faber and Krieg 2002). Economic and racial segregation across different cities and towns creates unequal capacities across these different communities. For instance, in the twentieth century, the Black population was tightly concentrated in Boston proper, particularly in neighborhoods like Roxbury, Dorchester, the South End, and Mattapan. Given increasing costs of housing, the Black population has been shifting to other communities in the Metro area; in 2020, 64% of Black residents in Greater Boston (including those identifying as multiracial and Latino) lived outside the city, while the city's Black population began declining after 2000 (Ciurczak et al. 2023). This suburbanization, however, is highly racially segregated; Black homeowners have concentrated in just a few communities, including Brockton, Randolph, and Taunton (Cornelissen and Godinez-Puig 2023). Racial segregation has lessened across the Metro area as its population has diversified, according to a 2025 analysis by the Boston Foundation, but segregation by income has grown, especially among high-income households clustering in high-income neighborhoods (Martin et al. 2025).

While the cities and towns in the Boston metropolitan region share many vulnerabilities to climate impacts, they do not necessarily prioritize climate action in the same way. Municipal independence allows some communities to blaze new paths in adopting climate-friendly policies, but it also leaves a patchwork of approaches to climate mitigation. There is currently no overarching authority for implementing climate adaptation projects that cross municipal boundaries, and any climate-related disaster affecting the metro area would be met with multiple emergency response systems that may lack coordination. Moreover, many communities of Greater Boston lack the capacity for climate adaptation planning and implementation that the city has, laying the groundwork for uneven climate risks and responses to exacerbate spatial inequalities.

Economic Development

Though Boston now ranks as one of the country's major technology centers, the city is just decades out from a reinvention that once seemed improbable. Once ranked one of the country's most distressed cities in the 1970s, Boston rapidly escaped the downward pull of economic decline that still plagued some of the country's older industrial cities at the turn of the millennium. The city's history is filled with such reinventions, as its leaders have struggled to maintain or revitalize the urban economy. Boston has never been able to rely on abundant natural resources and other geographical advantages for its competitive success. Instead, it has relied on economic diversity to reconfigure its economy to respond to technological shifts and economic trends. As Glaeser (2003) has argued, Boston's human capital allowed it to reinvent itself several times: from a colonial port to a hub of seafaring expertise in the late eighteenth century, to an industrial and manufacturing center in the nineteenth century, and to a growing metropolis in the late twentieth century powered by finance, health care, technology, and professional services. It regained its economic foothold by providing the right skills and services at the right time.

Boston flourished as a postcolonial trade center and later as a mercantile hub for regional textile manufacturing by inserting itself into global trade networks. Boston's economy diversified by the middle of the nineteenth century, with the city becoming a center for banking, insurance, and publishing. These new industries, combined with Boston's significant educational infrastructure, helped to lay the groundwork for a revival after its port gradually lost ground to other East Coast ports. It suffered from a period of economic decline in the twentieth century as New England's textile industry vanished as manufacturing moved to the South and later overseas.

By the 1980s, the Boston metropolitan area experienced an economic expansion that was popularly called the "Massachusetts Miracle," which brought a low unemployment rate and high per capita income to a state that had seemed hopelessly mired in economic decline (Tager 1991). The region benefited from federal Cold War-era funding for research and development in defense technology, with economic growth flowing from its considerable strengths in university research labs at Harvard and MIT. The region also grew in the business and financial services sectors. In this case, the turnaround was not located in the city proper but in the larger metropolitan area, with spatial investments from economic development radiating away from the city along the Route 128 corridor. Highway construction policy encouraged this outflow, as the Massachusetts Turnpike and Central Artery enabled suburban development by speeding commutes to the city (O'Connell 2013).

Greater Boston's educational infrastructure provides a deep pool of technical, professional, and design expertise that helps to foster innovation and opportunity. The metropolitan area has a long history of active leadership in both the public and private sectors around planning and improving the city, which can be seen today in the many institutions contributing research, analysis, and implementation of action around climate change. With nearly 140,000 students in the city of Boston alone, 39% of residents are between the ages of 18 and 34 (City of Boston 2022a). Boston is one of the largest biotech hubs in the world, home to some of the most recognizable hospitals and world-class medical research centers, while Massachusetts provides 23% of the biopharma research and development workforce in the United States.

The fruits of this trend can be seen today in Boston's recent population growth, economic investment in biotechnology and laboratory space, and new construction. According to the U.S. Bureau of Economic Analysis, the Boston metropolitan statistical area (which extends into southern New Hampshire) represents the eighth-largest metropolitan economy in the United States by gross domestic product (GDP). But new investments in old neighborhoods can also bring negative consequences for residents. In 2020, Boston was ranked by the National Community Reinvestment Coalition as the third most "intensely gentrified" city in the United States, behind San Francisco-Oakland and Denver, and the city has experienced growing income inequality (Figure 3.4). While many cities and towns across the country struggle with continued

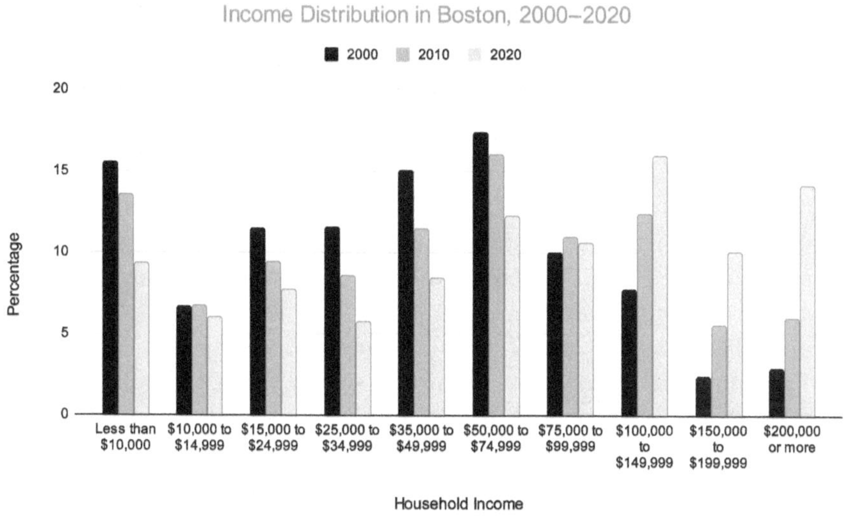

Figure 3.4 Income Distribution in Boston, 2000–2020

poverty and disinvestment, Boston is one of a small subset experiencing dramatic gentrification among low- and moderate-income communities and displacement of longstanding residents (Richardson et al. 2019). These forces have changed the visible character and demographics of numerous neighborhoods of Boston, including historically white ethnic neighborhoods, neighborhoods of color, and areas with large immigrant populations.

This recent upward economic trajectory, however, has been modulated first by the COVID-19 pandemic and then by an increasingly uncertain economy. Like many cities, Boston shed jobs and businesses during the pandemic, and its office space has the highest vacancy rate in decades, particularly in the downtown area and among older office buildings. A continuing dependence on the biotech sector for growth makes the city increasingly vulnerable to downturns in life sciences investment (Fahey 2022). Indeed, a recent downturn in Boston's commercial real estate market has generated fears that the city may fall prey to an "urban doom loop" that could make tech centers like San Francisco, Seattle, and Boston vulnerable to rapid post-pandemic economic downturns (Gupta et al. 2022; Nanos 2023). This fear has been heightened by recent actions and policies of the Trump administration, including the withdrawal of federal support for research that has fueled large parts of Greater Boston's economy. In addition to the broader threats to Boston's overall adaptive capacity, federal pullbacks pose direct threats to climate action in Boston and its larger region, stalling momentum for offshore wind and solar energy, environmental justice programs, and climate change adaptation.

Boston's Adaptive Capacity Today

According to the SETS framework, interactions between different dimensions of an urban system can impact the state of the system and therefore its adaptive capacity in the face of climate change (Markolf et al. 2018). While SETS are complex systems in a dynamic state of interaction, histories of urban development can help disentangle system dynamics over time by tracing a limited set of interacting conditions, actors, and physical features. Applying a SETS perspective to the history of Boston's development underscores how urban decision-making in the past was frequently prompted by impacts and feedback between socioeconomic, ecological, and technological elements of the urban system. I have highlighted how infrastructural interventions in Boston have often been designed to respond to social-ecological problems generated by urban development. In Figure 3.5, I depict conceptually how an ecological impact on the social dimension in the SETS (such as growing pollution) at one time point leads to a social response to create new infrastructure, which then changes the conditions of the SETS at a later time point and has both intended and unintended impacts on ecological and social dimensions. Any domain of the urban system can be subject to cycles of improvement, transformation, disinvestment, and stagnation. These new changing conditions then guide the adaptive pathway of the system.

Boston's history provides examples of flexibly adapting to new conditions and opportunities in the past that bode well for meeting the challenges of climate change. Beyond offering a portrait of Boston's climate-related context, the history described here highlights three broader points that are relevant to other urban systems.

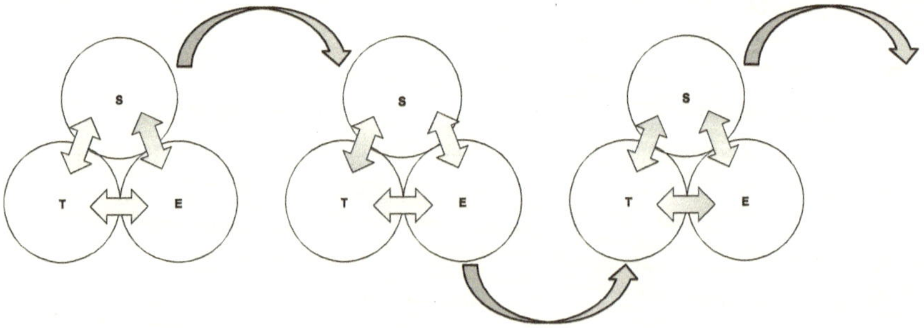

Figure 3.5 The SETS framework can be used to "disentangle" urban system dynamics over time.

Legacy effects

Entrenched social patterns and divisions clearly shape the landscape of vulnerability to climate change. Past cycles of urban immigration, political conflict, and elite-driven suburbanization have shaped the physical landscape of the city, creating its overall radiating pattern of density. At the same time, longstanding public and private disinvestment in certain neighborhoods that have also contributed a heterogenous landscape of risks and vulnerabilities within this spatial pattern. Spatial patterns of risk that we see in Boston do not clearly fall along lines of income, race, or other social vulnerabilities. Instead, the landscape is shaped by "legacy effects" like those described by Grove et al. (2018) in Baltimore, in which historical patterns of inequality and decision-making create complex patterns of environmental amenities and disamenities that have implications for sustainable urban transitions. Looking ahead, we can expect to see similarly complex patterns of change as forces such as inequality, gentrification, public and private investment, and economic instability interact with climate change across the urban landscape.

SETS "entanglement"

Literature on SETS governance emphasizes the possibilities for greater interconnection of SETS dimensions (McPhearson et al. 2021b). Chester et al. (2023) argue that fostering resilience in urban SETS requires shifting governance from an ethos of control to one of "sensemaking" that considers the complex and entangled nature of social, ecological, and technological aspects of urban systems. While the utility of "entanglement" as a factor in urban decision-making remains to be explored, Boston's history illustrates how a deeper awareness of interconnection of social, ecological, and technological factors in decision-making has emerged over time in North American cities. The development of urban infrastructure—water, sewage treatment and disposal, and transportation—has driven the creation of new metropolitan governance systems and institutions. As these systems have encountered new and increasingly complex problems, urban sensemaking has adapted. Social activism and institution-building have helped to bring social and ecological values into infrastructural decisions and to create more complex governance, such as the multilevel governance systems that evolved through the Boston Harbor Clean-Up. Thus, a historical perspective suggests that entanglement of social and ecological values in decision-making is an emergent quality that arises from the dynamic interactions of urban system dimensions and conditions.

Scale of SETS governance

Boston's history illustrates the importance of *scale* when conceptualizing an urban SETS. While we might imagine a bounded system drawn by municipal border, Boston shows that decision-making within the larger metropolitan SETS sometimes takes place at scales mismatched to the urban ecological and social problems to be addressed. Given Greater Boston's size, complexity, and political fragmentation, the scale of governance is an ever-present aspect of debate in addressing metropolitan problems such as environmental degradation, economic inequality, and housing affordability. Scale of governance is and will continue to be a major issue in mitigating and adapting to climate change, particularly when energy systems and other infrastructures rely on cross-boundary adaptation. In Boston's past, urban infrastructure has often driven new metropolitan governance systems; similarly, addressing climate change mitigation and adaptation may require new approaches to metropolitan governance that allow for greater entanglement of distinct institutions and entities within a larger urban SETS.

Chapter 4

BOSTON'S CLIMATE ACTION EVOLUTION

The presence of champions, including mayoral leadership, is a crucial factor in advancing new climate policies. Boston has displayed a notable consistency in its commitments to climate action, stemming in part from political continuity (the city has had only three elected mayors in the past three decades and one acting mayor who served for eight months before the current mayor was elected in 2021) and political homogeneity, as the city has had Democratic mayors for nearly a century, and its city council is firmly Democratic. These mayors, though distinct in their leadership style and policies, have consistently acknowledged climate change as a problem, positioned the city as a climate leader, incorporated climate science into planning and policies, engaged in national and international climate networks, and enacted some of the most progressive climate policies and programs in the nation.

But the municipal government's approach to climate action has also evolved, and this chapter examines this evolution, focusing particularly on a study of its climate actions plans. As a city that has been solidly supportive of sustainability for decades, Boston offers an example of how the expectations for urban leadership around climate planning and policy have changed and deepened over time. Environmental advocates might argue that the city has not evolved rapidly or profoundly enough to meet the current situation. This is not a problem unique to Boston; many cities face the challenge of turning early leadership on climate into a more profound transformation to meet stated goals and emissions targets. Thus Boston, though shaped by its own unique local politics and context, is illustrative of larger trends in urban climate policy, and offers lessons in both its successes and shortcomings.

First Climate Action Plan (2007): Taking Stock

Climate policy in Boston began under its influential mayor from 2003 to 2014, Thomas H. Menino. During the long Menino administration, the City of Boston took increasingly decisive steps toward acknowledging climate change. Boston can claim to have followed a Climate Action Plan since 2007, with an updated plan issued every three to four years since that time. Up to this time, much of what could be considered climate action fell under the umbrella of sustainability and "green" policy, without setting explicit goals related to climate change mitigation or adaptation. The first plan was a simple document that explained what was known about sources of greenhouse gas emissions in the city and described key initiatives up to that time (City of Boston 2007). It was less a plan of action than a progress report of the city's sustainability actions to date (Bassett and Shandas 2010). A lengthy introduction was devoted to explaining the greenhouse effect and basic information about climate change and justifying climate action, reflecting how novel municipal climate action was as a policy priority at the time.

The accounting of the city's climate work focused on five categories—buildings and other structures, energy sources, transportation, waste management, and land use—and consisted of programs and pilot projects that were limited in scope. For instance, efforts to reduce emissions related to buildings—then estimated to account for 78% of the city's total emissions—centered on a strategy of lowering energy consumption across municipal-owned buildings by 10%. The city's two largest emitters—the Boston Housing Authority and the Boston Public Schools—had engaged in a variety of energy efficiency programs, and the city had supported other efficiency-related actions, such as installing LED traffic lights. The document demonstrates limited overall strategy, coordination, and planning; it depicts a city that has opportunistically taken actions that represent sustainability but has not yet created any kind of organized plan or governance structure around climate change. It lacked specific sustainability targets and governance structures for coordinating or evaluating the effectiveness of interventions.

An accompanying executive order by Mayor Menino called on the city to reduce municipal greenhouse gas emissions by 7% below 1990 levels by 2012, and by 80% by 2050, making it one of the more ambitious long-term mitigation goals from cities around the country (Wheeler 2008). Menino also called for an integrated plan to "reduce the risks from the likely effects of climate change" and mandated that city agencies include climate change projections in their planning and permitting review processes (Menino 2007). Boston was notable as the first city to incorporate LEED green building standards into its building codes (Wheeler, 2008), although the implementation of this standard did not actually require that buildings obtain LEED certification.

A review of U.S. cities' climate action plans at this time found that many were innovative on a local level—they represented a new "first" for city government—rather than representing overall policy innovations (Bassett and Shandas 2010). Many action plans simply took the steps of acknowledging climate change as a municipal priority and setting up a framework for continued dialogue and action, rather than launching innovative policies or programs. Boston's first action plan also said very little about climate adaptation, which also mirrored a lagging trend of interest in adapting cities to climate impacts (Bulkeley 2010).

2011 Climate Action Plan Update: Setting Targets

In 2009, with the support of private foundation grants, Menino formed a Climate Action Leadership Committee—consisting largely of representatives from business, science, and prominent nonprofits—and a Community Advisory Committee with representatives of local neighborhoods—to create a set of recommendations for the city's next goals, policies, and initiatives around climate change. This approach of creating stakeholder groups was an important tactic for drawing a small but committed group of residents into the climate planning process (Anguelovski and Carmin 2011). The committees issued a report in 2010, "Sparking Boston's Climate Revolution," that argued for a "bold" leap ahead in the city's responses to climate change. (Lubber and Hunt 2010). It also advocated adopting the state's climate mitigation goal of reducing emissions by 80% by 2050, with an accelerated interim target 25% by 2020. The report also included innovative recommendation, such as establishing a process to collect and analyze new data in its adaptation planning, creating a public commission to engage community members, and promoting economic equity to avoid distributive injustices in climate change's burdens and benefits.

The city adopted these recommendations as the outline of its 2011 Climate Action Plan Update (City of Boston 2011). The 2011 plan adopted the "80 by 2050" target and set an interim goal of reducing greenhouse gas emissions by 25% in 2020. The report provided detailed emissions reductions targets across a range of sectors and set 2020 goals for each sector, reflecting a more organized approach to climate mitigation that went far beyond the accounting of the previous plan.

The plan acknowledged the city had not yet made clear progress on reducing emissions beyond fluctuations due to the 2009 economic recession (City of Boston 2011). The rationale for mitigating climate change focused on local and regional economic benefits and new job opportunities. To achieve its 2020 emissions goals, the plan proposed an array of strategies, each anticipated to make a small contribution to the larger whole. As such, the plan does not read as transformative so much as taking a surgical approach to improving the efficiency of city operations. This approach was in keeping with Menino's characterization as an "urban mechanic" intent on fixing problems in the city in a targeted way (Seelye 2014).

Adaptation planning during this time had become a growing focus in many urban policies globally, though U.S. cities generally lagged behind European cities in shifting from governance focused on mitigation to integrating adaptation (Aylett 2015). By 2011, climate impacts—particularly sea-level rise—were gaining urgency among Boston's nonprofit and academic circles. The city was also involved in state-level policy discussions about climate adaptation (City of Boston 2011). Like many cities, Boston had not yet institutionalized climate adaptation policy (Anguelovski and Carmin 2011), and the 2010 "Sparking Boston's Climate Revolution" report called on the city to make adaptation an equal priority as mitigation. The 2011 CAP update reflected this emerging focus, emphasizing that adaptation should be a priority equal to mitigation and incorporated into all planning initiatives and activities, but it did not provide detailed plans to do so.

In spite of the involvement of a stakeholder group in shaping policy, the report was largely technocratic and left out a fundamental piece of the puzzle: residents. Although acknowledging the need for engagement around climate change, examples of such opportunities emphasized existing avenues of participation such as city council hearing and improving education and climate change awareness rather than soliciting direct participation in planning. This language reflected an environment in which climate change was still highly disputed, even in liberal bastions like Boston, and a culture that saw climate change action as a largely scientific, technical, and economic problem, requiring government to partner with experts and business, but not necessarily social transformation.

Greenovate Climate Action Plan Update (2014): Civic Climate Engagement

When the second update to the city's action plan arrived in 2014, Boston had experienced its first change in mayoral leadership in two decades. Martin J. "Marty" Walsh became mayor that year and included climate change initiatives as a priority. Despite this change, the 2014 update was largely a continuation of the previous plan, with several improvements and shifts in emphasis. Importantly, it reflected a growing emphasis on quantitative measurement of climate emissions in broader discussions of urban climate change governance (City of Boston 2014). It included more rigorous citywide emissions estimates, specific targets for meeting the goal of an 80% emissions reduction by 2080, and a more targeted focus on climate change preparedness (it also provided the first measurements of progress: Boston's citywide emissions had dropped 17% and city government emissions had dropped almost 25% since 2005).

The update also brought a novel emphasis on community engagement, representing a shift from climate mitigation and adaptation as a purely governmental and expert domain toward a more inclusive process. The new action plan was released as part of a broader "Greenovate" initiative that emphasized civic participation, social priorities, and adaptation alongside climate change mitigation. Key goals of the 2014 Greenovate Climate Action Plan Update were reducing emissions, promoting healthy and equitable communities, measuring progress and performance, preparing for climate impacts, and increasing community engagement (City of Boston 2014). Through the Greenovate program, the city launched several initiatives aimed at engaging citizens in climate work, including training "Greenovate Leaders" to lead community-level public conversations about climate change.

Climate Ready Boston (2016): Comprehensive Adaptation Planning

Although Boston's 2011 action plan had promised comprehensive adaptation planning, the city's approach to climate impacts was still piecemeal. Developers in areas of high flood risk, for instance, had begun to be asked by the Boston Redevelopment Authority to elevate buildings on an ad hoc basis. Boston's near miss from major impacts of Hurricane Sandy in October 2012 sparked interest in waterfront climate adaptation, particularly among powerful members of the local business community and nonprofit sectors, putting new pressures on the city to make climate adaptation a greater focus of its agenda. Under the Walsh administration, Boston developed an increasingly robust planning response for climate adaptation, particularly in response to sea-level rise. Climate adaptation became more prominent in the city's planning and public outreach, driven in part by outside private funding and a growing urgency among the city's business, nonprofit, and academic circles. The Green Ribbon Commission, a climate-focused business group, provided the impetus and financial support in 2015 to launch Climate Ready Boston, a broad strategic planning initiative focusing on data collection, vulnerability analysis, and then neighborhood-level planning for key vulnerable neighborhoods (City of Boston 2016).

The release of the City's Climate Ready Boston report in 2016 marked a turning point in the response to climate risks. It included the comprehensive assessment of Boston's climate risks from the Boston Research Advisory Group (BRAG) described in Chapter 2. Climate Ready Boston also included a vulnerability assessment of risks associated with three climate hazards (extreme heat, stormwater flooding, and coastal and riverine flooding); an analysis of eight focus areas with high vulnerability, including the South

Boston Waterfront; and a set of initiatives and an implementation roadmap for improving climate resilience (City of Boston 2016). Climate Ready Boston is not just a single report but a multiyear initiative and planning process. In the years following the report, a set of neighborhood-level planning processes has developed more detailed plans for climate adaptation in vulnerable neighborhoods. While the initiative considers broad climate change impacts, neighborhood-level planning has focused on flood risks along the waterfront, and the proposed changes largely involve building up or out along the shoreline to protect the built environment and support plans for continued waterfront development and growth.

2019 to Present: Planning for Carbon-Free Equity

Under the Walsh administration, the city accelerated its carbon emissions goals and took steps to recognize racial and economic equity as key elements of Boston's climate change response. It set an intermediate goal of 50% reduction of citywide carbon emissions (over a 2005 baseline) by 2030. In 2017, Walsh set a new goal of carbon neutrality by 2050 (City of Boston 2019). In addition to these citywide goals, Boston also pledged to reduce municipal emissions 60% by 2030. Boston's 2019 Climate Action Plan Update, released under the Walsh administration, detailed strategies to "accelerate Boston's progress" to meet its first carbon reduction goals, now just over a decade away. The 2019 update advocated taking direct steps to reduce carbon emissions across the city but also voiced support for carbon offsets for the remaining emissions (City of Boston 2019). The update placed a greater emphasis on social equity than previous iterations of the plan.

As in many cities, the conversation around equity—particularly racial equity and economic inequality—became more acute during Black Lives Matter protests and the COVID-19 pandemic. In Boston, this conversation was heightened when City Council president Kim Janey became Acting Mayor after Walsh was appointed to the Biden administration, giving Boston both its first Black and first woman mayor. Michelle Wu, who prevailed over Janey in the 2021 mayoral election, brought an ambitious and wide-ranging Green New Deal (GND) platform for Boston. The GND began as in the United States as a failed congressional resolution, but it has become an internationally recognized policy framework. Like the national Green New Deal, her platform included social equity as a central aspect of climate action, such as promoting economic development by engaging a "green work force" to create and maintain new climate-adaptive infrastructure. Wu's overwhelming electoral victory represented a shift to the left for a city that had often favored establishment mayors and lifted a key obstacle that prevented the city's increasingly progressive City Council from advancing social and environmental justice agendas.

Earlier initiatives such as Greenovate and Climate Ready Boston have continued, but the city's planning has shifted focus (see Chapter 4 for an extended discussion on the city's recent climate adaptation and equity strategies). Under Wu, Boston has issued several planning documents highlighting climate justice, including plans addressing heat resilience and urban forestry, which will be described in later sections. Boston's Climate Action Plan for 2030 is in draft form only as of this writing and scheduled to be finalized by late 2025. The exact strategies and programs are still unclear: the draft includes a long menu of ideas to be decided on with public input. But the plan is still illuminating in its succinct set of overarching goals in three categories: carbon emissions reduction, climate resilience, and climate justice. It is described as being "grounded in climate justice" and brings mitigation, adaptation, and equity into a united climate action plan for the first time (City of Boston 2025, 3). The plan maintains the emissions goals set by the previous administration but finds that the city would cut its emissions 44% (over a 2005 baseline) by 2030 if it meets existing targets, leaving a 6% gap to reach its goal of 50% reduction in emissions by that time. The plan outlines strategies for meeting its existing targets and identifying additional areas for reductions to make up the gap. Under climate resilience, the focus is shifting from planning to implementation, addressing a serious gap in strategies that have been proposed and those that have been funded and created. Under climate justice, the plan proposes a set of principles for guiding climate work and calls for a clearer definition of environmental justice communities in Boston.

From a "Climate Mechanic" to the Green New Deal

Boston has benefited from leadership that has consistently embraced climate action over the past two decades, avoiding a loss of continuity in programs and climate commitments. All recent mayors have served as leaders in national and international climate networks and have prioritized climate action within city government. The evolution of Boston's climate action plans, then, is representative of broader trends in the science and social acceptance of climate change and shifting urban climate politics in the United States. Three aspects of this evolution stand out.

One is the deepening of climate commitments as the city has set more ambitious emissions goals. In Boston's first climate action plans, we can see an example of a broader trend of cities taking an opportunistic approach to climate action through 'governance alternatives'—including financing innovations, certification and benchmarking programs such as LEED and Energy Star, and climate action challenges—without developing a broader organizational agenda for climate change mitigation and adaptation (van der Heijden 2021a). These plans reflect an incremental, domain-limited, and technocratic approach to addressing climate action, with the municipal government taking a role as "climate mechanic," fixing urban unsustainability by making targeted improvements to aspects of urban infrastructure and processes. Tracking emissions and setting ambitious climate targets has forced cities to develop a more comprehensive portfolio of strategies that embed climate action into all levels of government. Adaptation planning, meanwhile, has shifted from visioning and planning to project financing and implementation.

A second aspect is a change in policy agendas and discourses from sustainability to resilience to climate justice, reflecting the merging awareness of climate-related risks, the social impacts of climate change, and climate-related social inequities. Some of the city's early efforts on adaptation to sea-level rise, paid short shrift to inequities that may result from adaptation projects, but current policies are attempting to recenter the city's focus on socially vulnerable neighborhoods like East Boston. While all climate action plans emphasize the benefits of sustainability to society and the economy, social equity becomes a major focus of recent climate planning documents, which acknowledge the potential negative social consequences of climate action as well as touting economic and social benefits.

Finally, planning in Boston has shifted toward a more systemic approach to addressing climate change through policy. Earlier action plans emphasize technological and ecological interventions to improve the city's carbon footprint guided by technocratic planning processes, while later plans increasingly emphasize resident engagement and community involvement. After largely separating climate mitigation from adaptation, Boston's newest plan integrates them into one document. Returning to the characterization of Boston as an urban SETS, the evolution of climate action in the city can also be viewed as representing an increasing embeddedness of social, technological, and ecological dimensions of the city into planning (Chester et al. 2023). Boston's GND is characterized by an integrated approach to economic growth and technological development that is guided by ecological sustainability, decarbonization of the economy, and social justice (Barbier 2010). In this sense, the GND platform acknowledges the increasingly entangled relationships between environmental, economic, technological, and social changes in cities pursuing just climate transitions.

Chapter 5

BOSTON'S CLIMATE GOVERNANCE: A NEGOTIATED PATH

Governing urban climate change mitigation and adaptation require engaging nongovernmental actors, including neighborhood-level organizations, nonprofits and special-interest groups, private companies and business groups, and private funders. Progress is shaped by state policies, regional and metropolitan politics, and numerous actors working within the city. This dispersion of power across various actors (including local, regional, and national governments; residents; non-governmental organizations; private businesses; and supra-national networks and institutions) is often called multilevel governance. In the urban literature, multilevel governance studies often focus on understanding the relative roles of vertical hierarchies of state and city governments and horizontal city-to-city networks such as national or transnational urban networks like C40 Cities in advancing climate action (Bulkeley 2010; Lee and Koski 2015). While multilevel governance implies a decentralization of typical hierarchies of power, there are usually strong constraints and challenges for this kind of decentralization, given existing legal mandates, regulatory structures, and entrenched processes. Coordination between multiple actors can help create policy interventions that are mutually reinforcing and supporting (Allain-Dupré 2020).

In this chapter, I briefly describe the various levels of climate governance in Boston, including actors and institutions in the government and outside it. While we may think of municipal governments as a single entity, they contain a multiplicity of entities and processes across the mayor's office, administrative departments, various boards and commissions, and city council. Within the city, many non-governmental actors have worked to enable and accelerate climate action in Boston, including local and national non-profit organizations, businesses, academic and philanthropic institutions, and citizen activists. The city government often sets a policy agenda, provides funding, and acts as a coordinator and hub within this larger network of actors. Finally, the federal and state government and other regional actors, such as utilities, impact a city's ability to execute a climate action agenda.

By reviewing some of these key actors, I aim to connect the concept of multilevel governance to issues raised earlier in the discussion of urban SETS. Many of the steps the city has taken toward climate action would be impossible without higher levels of government, non-governmental institutions, and resident groups. Boston's adaptation and mitigation pathways are in many ways determined and advanced by these various factions. The Boston area nurtures a strong collaborative learning ecosystem around climate change through academic, private, and government partnerships. These actors work together to forge a negotiated adaptation pathway—at best, working collectively toward a just transition. At times, however, governance of a particular issue is fragmented across multiple actors with different aims and/or jurisdictions. This fragmentation can be viewed in one perspective as an opportunity for locally driven, democratic, and nimble decision-making (Ostrom 1972) and by another perspective as a cause of spatial segregation and unfair land use policies (Lowery 2000). Examples of fragmentation in climate planning are relevant to these longstanding debates about metropolitan governance, but they also raise the question of how to improve integration of governance between different SETS domains across different administrative and spatial scales within the city of Boston and its larger metropolitan area.

Municipal Government

Within the municipal government, elected politicians define policy challenges and goals and craft solutions, but the administration implements and stewards those goals and solutions (Hofstad and Vedeld 2021). Nearing two decades from its first organized climate action plan, the city of Boston has now fully institutionalized climate change into its administration and policies. Whereas Boston's early climate actions were highly dependent on executive orders and new plans, climate change mitigation and preparedness are now embedded in the administrative goals and functions of numerous agencies in the city. The urban GND is often described as a series of progressive policies. Looking at Boston's implementation of the GND, however, underscores the importance of a broader administrative reorganization in achieving the stated aims of the GND.

Much of the official responsibility for climate change action in the city's administration has been housed in its Environment, Energy and Open Space Cabinet, a cabinet that has changed names and duties slightly since it was created in 2006 but which now oversees several city departments as well as regulating bodies like the Conservation Commission, which enforces the state's Wetlands Protection Act at the municipal level. The Environment cabinet typically serves as the "face" of climate action in the city. Many city agencies, however, are also involved in aspects of the city's climate response, including Public Works, Emergency Management, Public Utilities, a Resilience and Racial Equity Department, and the Boston Public Health Commission. The Wu administration has systematically expanded the city's climate-focused administration in the municipal government. The city has hired a Director of Carbon Neutrality and other staff to oversee its building decarbonization efforts. The city has hired a Director of Green Infrastructure—making Boston the first major city in the United States to create an executive-level position overseeing green infrastructure implementation—as well as other staff to support a more robust green infrastructure program. Structural changes to Boston's administration have also created positions with explicitly linked environmental and social goals, such as an Office of Food Justice, as well as a Green New Deal Director who coordinates climate action with goals of social equity and economic justice.

Boston has also taken recent steps to create more integrated governance in its climate adaptation planning and infrastructure building. While the city has a well-established adaptation planning program with Climate Ready Boston, it is not always clear how adaptation projects would be implemented, as broad resilience strategies created by the Environment Department ultimately must be executed by other departments (Fitzgerald et al. 2022). This lack of clear coordination in implementation represents a potential challenge in the city's efforts to govern interventions in the urban SETS in an integrated way. In 2024, the city created a new department, the Office of Climate Resilience, within the Environment, Energy, and Open Space cabinet to oversee resilience efforts and accelerate the city's progress in implementing projects.

The municipal government also includes an elected city council that represents neighborhood-level interests and advances new local legislation. Boston is governed by a so-called strong mayor-council system, in which the mayor has a high level of autonomy, administrative authority, and budgetary control over the city, and can veto city council votes. In 2021, Boston voters approved an amendment that gives some budgetary power to the council, allowing it to veto a mayor's budget and propose amendments. In general, however, City Council members have limited powers over municipal administration. They do, however, help drive constituent agendas, including climate action, through legislation and by advocating at both the local and state levels.

Members in the City Council have advanced several resolutions and pieces of landmark legislation that have addressed climate change. In 2017, the Council passed a resolution committing Boston to the goals of the Paris Agreement, and in 2019, the Council passed a resolution in favor of the Green New Deal, spearheaded by then-Councilor Michelle Wu. Recent legislation includes a local wetlands ordinance designed to both protect local habitats and promote climate change adaptation (also spearheaded by Wu's office), an ordinance requiring large buildings to meet emissions caps and achieve net zero emissions by 2050 (BERDO 2.0, which will be discussed in the following chapter), and a stricter energy code for buildings in the city.

Planning and development in Boston

Boston's efforts to reduce emissions and improve the resilience of built environment must be considered in the context of the city's overall approach to development. The Boston Planning and Development Agency (BPDA, formerly the Boston Redevelopment Authority or BRA) has shaped Boston's modern economic development and its built environment. Its role in the city has been controversial; it was "rebranded" from its previous moniker in part to shake connotations of top-down planning during the urban renewal era. The agency is a separate legal entity created by state legislation with greater power than a city department. As a City Council member, Michelle Wu proposed to "abolish" the BPDA (Wu 2019), given its history of poor community engagement and lack of accountability, a move that would require legislation at the state level. As Mayor, she created a separate Planning Department to "restore planning as a core function of City government" and filed a home-rule petition with the state narrowing the BPDA's scope to three principles—resiliency, affordability, and equity—rather than urban renewal functions.

Massachusetts is a "non-plan" state that does not require land use regulations to be consistent with comprehensive plans (Curtin 2005). Boston has a history of not engaging in comprehensive planning, instead taking a piecemeal approach to development and relying on the power of the BRA/BPDA as a negotiation. For instance, many larger developments are zoned as Planned Development Areas, akin to creating a special zoning district for a specific project. Boston uses Planned Development Areas as part of a value creation strategy; developers are allowed to build higher, denser (and more valuable) buildings than the zoning code allows in exchange for public benefits (Kim 2020). Compared to other major US cities, Boston has had a high proportion of projects that are up-zoned through a negotiation process rather than being planned from the outset (Kim 2020). After the 1960s, master planning in the city was absent, until Imagine Boston 2030 became the first master plan in 50 years (City of Boston 2017a). Such plans are not legally binding, however. The flexibility of such an approach comes at the cost of transparency, accountability, and consistency in planning (Curtin 2005).

As the overseer of new development, the BPDA has had an important role in advancing Boston's climate mitigation and adaptation goals, particularly by incorporating energy efficiency and resilience into the BPDA's Article 80 Development Review process. These functions now lie under the new Planning Department. Some of the new department's goals are to update the zoning code to allow for more housing and mixed-use spaces, increase affordable housing, and make the Article 80 process more transparent. A citywide Planning Advisory Council is charged with better coordinating planning goals across city departments.

Philanthropic Institutions

Discussions of urban public–private partnerships often focus on the construction of public urban infrastructure and provision of formerly public services through private sector participation (Koppenjan and Enserink 2009), while municipal governments are often credited with setting policy agenda and creating their own plans through public engagement processes. In Boston, however, private institutions not only shape the provision of infrastructure but also the conception and design of climate policy in municipal government. Private funding lies behind nearly every city-led report or initiative related to climate change. Private foundations, business groups, and nonprofits also help to drive the agenda of municipal climate responses, particularly in adaptation planning on Boston's waterfront, which is the site of intense real estate development and public interest. These organizations, though not formally aligned with the city, have also funded key city initiatives, as well as sponsoring independent programs and reports that advance climate action work by other nonprofit institutions and improve the accountability of municipal climate action.

The Barr Foundation, a locally based private foundation created by billionaire Amos Barr Hostetter, Jr., has been instrumental in bringing climate change into the city's agenda and enabling climate planning and action to the government and non-governmental organizations across the city. The Barr Foundation has funded arts and educational programs in Boston since 1987 but began making its funding more visible and climate-focused after 2010. It has provided funding for most of the critical climate change reports, programs, and institutions discussed in this book.

The Boston Foundation is one of the oldest and largest locally focused private foundations in the country, is an important source of nonprofit grant making in the Greater Boston area (more than $175,000 in 2023) and partners with other institutions to create high-impact funds around particular issues. It focuses on improving social and economic equity, including environmental and climate justice issues, and it also supports research and monitoring of indicators of social and economic equity. Other private foundations, including the Sherry and Alan Leventhal Family Foundation, the Grantham Foundation, and the William and Flora Hewlett Foundation, have contributed to climate-related efforts like the Carbon Free Boston initiative. Foundations have sometimes funded work that holds government accountable for its planning, thus serving an important monitoring role in the city. For instance, the Barr Foundation helped the transportation nonprofit LivableStreets to independently assess the City's progress in achieving its targets set out in Go Boston 2030 (Gag 2020), and the Boston Foundation supported a progress report on Boston's emissions reductions goals (Fitzgerald et al. 2022).

Business and Real Estate

One of the most impactful organizations for climate in Boston is a public–private partnership called the Green Ribbon Commission (GRC), formed in 2011 as a group of civic and business leaders, co-chaired by the mayor, who would work closely with the city on its climate action plans. The GRC is a "voluntary CEO network" that was deliberately designed to be closely aligned with municipal government, and was created by then-Mayor Menino and Barr Foundation founder Hostetter (Mitic and White 2021). Remarkably, it was intended to serve as a supra-governmental force of climate governance that would "create political continuity across changes in administration," in Hostetter's words, ensuring that climate actions remained consistent with changes in mayoral leadership (Mitic and White 2021). It provided both the initial funding and planning leadership for Boston's Climate Ready Boston initiative and sponsored an influential weeklong European Climate Innovation Tour in 2016 that brought 25 leaders from the Boston area to learn about climate adaptation and mitigation projects in Amsterdam, Rotterdam, Copenhagen, and Malmo (Cleveland 2018). Since then, the GRC has provided financial support for numerous climate initiatives and sponsored reports on climate change in Boston, including partnering with the Boston Foundation's 2022 assessment of climate neutrality in Boston. It has served as an influential model for business-government collaboration for the City-Business Climate Alliance, an initiative that is working to nurture similar partnerships in cities around the world (City-Business Climate Alliance, n.d.). The GRC has adopted climate justice as one of its strategic goals, publicizing a report on the impacts of systemic racism on climate impacts in the city. The GRC also assists in climate action planning for local cultural and educational institutions. Other local business organizations include the Environmental Business Council, which partners with academic, private, and governmental organizations to sponsor forums for sharing knowledge about climate mitigation and adaptation strategies and practices, and A Better City, a business group originally created during Boston's "Big Dig" Central Artery project, which now advocates for building decarbonization and resiliency, among other issues.

Businesses in Boston are often partners in climate action, but not surprisingly, the local business sector has also served as a counter force in climate transitions. The city's powerful real estate industry, for instance, has been a major stakeholder in efforts to improve energy efficiency and resilience of buildings in Boston, both as individual developers and lobbying groups such as the Greater Boston Real Estate Board and NAIOP Massachusetts. While the groups have generally supported new climate regulation at the local and state level, they have pushed back against strict net-zero requirements for buildings and aspects of Boston's coastal flood regulation (Van Voorhis 2021; Banker & Tradesman 2024).

Nonprofit Organizations

Nonprofit organizations play a critical role in raising awareness and urgency around climate action in Boston, serving as voices of advocacy and as actors in climate change adaptation and mitigation measures, both alone and in partnership with the city, business, and other local institutions. Many of Boston's institutions with earlier origins in local environmental or social issues and have adopted climate change as an area of concern. For instance, Boston Harbor Now (which formed in 2016 from the merging of the Boston Harbor Association and Boston Harbor Island Alliance) has roots in advocacy around the federally mandated Boston Harbor cleanup project but more recently has advocated climate change adaptation and resilience on Boston's waterfront. Similarly, the Conservation Law Foundation of New England, which has fought for public access and benefits as Boston's waterfront has been redeveloped, has pushed for greater regulation of climate resilience. Other organizations have become climate advocates in part based on their locations, such as the waterfront-facing institutions New England Aquarium, Boston Children's Museum, and Museum of Science. National and local organizations focused on open space conservation such as the Trust for Public Land, the Trustees of Reservations, The Nature Conservancy, and Mass Audubon have also adopted climate change adaptation and mitigation as key areas of concern. Issue-focused nonprofits such as Livable Streets Alliance, Boston Cyclists Union, and Neighborhood of Affordable Housing, frequently serve as stakeholders in municipal planning processes around transportation and housing, which often overlap with climate issues. Non-profit groups sometimes take on the role of monitoring climate progress and holding government accountable for promised changes; for example, LivableStreets has been reporting on the City's progress on transportation goals.

Citizen Activists and Advocacy Groups

Despite the near-universal recognition of public engagement as a critical factor in climate change planning, discussions of urban governance sometimes overlook the vital role that organized citizen action plays in driving urban climate action—even when their engagement is not actively sought by government. In Boston, citizen activists, working individually and collectively in smaller nonprofits or informal action groups, have helped to shape climate polity. Many established foundations and nonprofits work as collaborative partners in municipal climate action. Numerous organizations also take on a more traditional role of public advocacy and activism, at times working in partnership with the city and at times pushing it to act further. For instance, the Boston Climate Action Network (BCAN), a local chapter of the Massachusetts Climate Action Network, formed in the early 2000s and has been involved in several climate action campaigns, including advocating for the Community Choice Electricity plan, state legislation to address natural gas leaks, and Boston's green building ordinance, and leading neighborhood-level educational programs for energy efficiency. Established groups like BCAN and the statewide organization Progressive Massachusetts also work with neighborhood-level progressive political and climate justice groups.

Collaborative governance of gas leaks

Massachusetts has one of the oldest natural gas distribution systems in the country, and it's been estimated that 2.7% of the natural gas distributed in Massachusetts is lost to leaks (McKain et al. 2015). The Boston area has seen a burgeoning activism around natural gas leaks that has led to substantial policy changes. From an urban SETS perspective, methane leaks highlight the embedded nature of urban environmental problems. The leaks represent a linked social and infrastructural problem caused by both the physical age of the system as well as its governance: as a largely hidden infrastructure that is managed by private utilities, gas infrastructure has suffered from a lack of political engagement, funding, and accountability to maintain and update it over time. In turn, methane leaks have environmental and social impacts: they contribute to climate change, degrade local air quality, and kill trees in the immediate vicinity of leaks by diffusing through soil. A statewide study found that environmental justice populations are disproportionately exposed to natural gas leaks and subjected to longer wait times for repair (Luna and Nicholas 2022).

Awareness of the magnitude of the problem began when a 2013 study identified more than 3,000 methane leaks across Boston (Phillips et al. 2013). The research spurred upwelling of interest in natural gas leaks from local officials and activist groups such as Mothers Out Front and led to immediate legislative action with a 2014 act that required utilities to disclose gas leaks for the first time. A subsequent study found that just 7% of the leaks in the Boston Metro area contribute about half of the volume of leaking gas; subsequent 2016 legislation required utilities to fix these leaks of significant environmental impact (SEIs). HEET, a nonprofit group focused on energy efficiency, began mapping the addresses of leaks across the state, making the leaks visible to the public (heet.org/who-we-are/about/). In 2019, HEET coordinated various stakeholders, including state legislators, activists, utilities, and academic researchers to create an innovative Shared Action Plan for addressing gas leaks, including gathering data on its effectiveness. HEET's preliminary findings reported a 46% reduction in SEI emissions between 2021 and 2024.

Methane leaks provide an example of how collaboration and mutualistic feedback between academic researchers, citizen activists, nonprofit groups, and legislators can lead to rapid and ongoing legislative action and policies to mitigate climate change. As depicted in Figure 5.1, this arrangement allows for input into decision-making from actors who interface with social, ecological, and technological dimensions of the issue. But there are also limits to collaborative and synergistic climate action that depend on a convergence of different interests, as different actors may have different visions for the future state of the SETS. Regulating gas leaks—a previously under-appreciated inefficiency in the state's gas distribution system—reduces emissions without threatening the primacy of natural gas in the state's energy system. Activists and environmental groups have harder struggle pushing an anti-gas agenda, such as blocking the construction of new pipelines and compressor stations. A progress report commissioned by Gas Leaks Allies argued that the state's program to fix gas leaks—the Gas System Enhancement Program (GSEP)—was only barely keeping up with the pace of new leaks, not making significant progress on improving the state's leaky system in alignment with the state's climate goals (Seavey 2021). The report called for rethinking the approach to the problem, redirecting money away from repairing the system and toward replacing it with renewable energy sources.

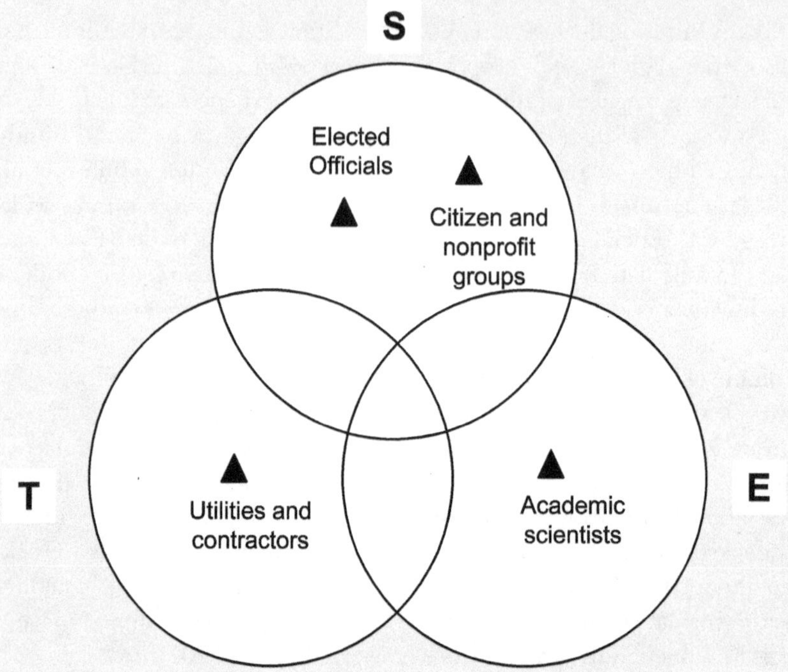

Figure 5.1 Collaborative governance of gas leaks as an example of SETS decision-making.

National and Transnational Networks

National and transnational municipal networks have been catalysts for urban climate action by spurring the exchange of information and sometimes direct financial support for urban climate action (Bulkeley 2010). Boston has taken a leading role in several national and international climate networks. It participates in the Urban Sustainability Directors Network (USDN), the Carbon Neutral Cities Network, as well as the C40 Cities network, which includes over 100 cities working together to limit their impacts on climate change. Former Mayor Walsh served as the North American co-chair for C40's Steering Committee, and Boston's 2019 Climate Action Plan is intended to be consistent with the C40 Cities' 2017 agenda, Deadline 2020, which sets a course for meeting targets under the Paris Agreement to limit global temperatures from rising more than 1.5°C (City of Boston 2019). Boston participates in the Urban Sustainability Directors' Network, Climate Mayors, and the Global Covenant of Mayors for Climate and Energy. Boston has also received financial support through the Bloomberg American Cities Climate Challenge.

Boston joined in the Rockefeller Foundation's 100 Resilient Cities initiative in 2014, a transnational municipal network that provided direct funding and consultancy services to municipal governments and was highly influential in promoting an urban resilience agenda before its abrupt end in 2019 (Nielsen and Papin 2021). In 2015, Boston hired its first Resilience Officer with funding from the 100 Resilient Cities program, choosing to focus on the roots of historical racism as key to its resilience (Stanley 2015). While this effort led to a citywide resilience strategy, one analysis found that it was politically motivated and largely reiterated existing policies rather than forwarding a transformative vision based on community engagement (van den Berg and Keenan 2019). Not all of the report's recommendations were followed, perhaps in part because its calls for systemic change were less accepted in 2017 than they are today (Reilly 2020). Mayor Walsh created a new Office of Equity in 2020, with a cabinet-level Chief of Equity, and with its Resilience and Racial Equity head now listed as a senior advisor to the cabinet, but the office has not played a leading role in climate change efforts across the city.

Under Michelle Wu, Boston is aligned ideologically with left-leaning Green New Deal movements that have been advanced on both a national and international level. Wu, however, has generally been less focused on prioritizing international knowledge exchange and leadership—missing the 2022 C40 World Mayors Summit, for instance (Lees 2023).

Private Consultancies

Private consultancies, engineering firms, and legal services play an underacknowledged role in government climate action at multiple scales (Christensen and Collington 2024). Private consultancies specializing in climate modeling, climate resilience analysis, urban design, and landscape architecture are indispensable for working alongside municipalities, nonprofits, and other institutions on climate data collection, planning, and project implementation. They can also act as de facto hubs for climate networks, serving as a conduit for exchange of ideas and the diffusion of best practices and standards across cities. Although typically seen as sources of technical expertise, consulting companies also help to shape policy by guiding municipalities and other organizations through planning processes and defining possible decisions and pathways. Major city plans and programs in Boston have relied on consulting companies such as Arcadis, Arup, Sasaki, SCAPE Landscape Architecture, Utile Architecture & Planning. Climate modeling by Woods Hole Group has been a fundamental technology for enabling the city's planning for sea-level rise. Often working relatively behind the scenes, these companies nevertheless have shaped the direction of major municipal actions like Climate Ready

Boston, and they bring technical expertise that underlies studies of Boston's emissions, adaptation strategies, and other climate-related issues. These private-sector actors tend to work closely with government groups and universities on projects that promote physical resilience, and are less involved in work that promotes social resilience and equity (Negrón et al. 2022).

Academic and Research Institutions

Research studies and planning tools developed in partnership with Boston's local universities and research institutions have been a major asset to the city and metropolitan area. Academic research, often in collaboration with private consultancies, has shed light on the city's greenhouse gas emissions, heat and flood risks, public health impacts, and other aspects of the urban environment. For instance, the Boston Research Advisory Group (BRAG) and Greater Boston Research Advisory Group (GBRAG), which include researchers at the University of Massachusetts Boston and other institutions and have provided the city with comprehensive information about local climate risks. The University of Massachusetts Boston engaged in a study of a proposed Harbor-Wide Barrier as a flood protection strategy with sea-level rise. University research is also critical for providing the data collection and analysis for policy documents that make strategic recommendations and provide accountability for the city's climate actions. Boston University's Institute for Sustainable Energy (now the Institute for Global Sustainability) worked with the Green Ribbon Commission to provide in-depth data collection and analysis on the City's greenhouse gas emissions, producing the Carbon Free Boston report in 2019 and a subsequent report on social equity. The Dukakis Center for Urban and Regional Policy at Northeastern University worked with the Boston Foundation to produce the Boston Climate Progress Report on the city's efforts to reach its emissions goals.

Collectively, schools and universities occupy 8.6% of Boston's land (Granberry et al. 2025). Given the large concentration of academic institutions in the Boston area, universities play a key role in the city and metropolitan area as landowners and stewards of the built environment. Several universities have been leaders in energy efficiency, including managing some of the oldest district energy systems in the country and investing in highly efficient buildings.

In addition to major reports and formal partnerships, the Boston area hosts a wide array of urban research as its large faculty and student population draws on the city as a subject and laboratory for research, either independently or in partnership with nonprofits and other institutions or community groups. An example of a promising community-based research project is C-HEAT, a research partnership between Boston University's School for Public Health and GreenRoots, a community organization in East Boston and the City of Chelsea, a two-year project funded by the Barr Foundation. The research team employed field studies and collaborative data collection techniques to study temperatures across Chelsea and East Boston and gather data on air conditioning and qualitative experiences of heat among residents (https://www.c-heatproject.org/). Another example of collaborative research is the Boston Area Research Initiative (BARI), which fosters community partnerships and offers research seed grants to projects that leverage data to examine civic-minded issues, including climate change.

Much academic research is short-term, however, which limits its impact. Research studies and academic projects are limited by grant funding cycles and the schedules of academic courses and design studios. As a wealth of ideas accumulates for how to solve urban challenges, the city lacks a mechanism to support longer-term engagement with academic researchers, foster sustained and ongoing monitoring programs, and more effectively harness the results of ongoing small-scale research projects, many of which result in a publication with no clear follow-up.

One potential model for the future is the Stone Living Lab, an innovative partnership between the City of Boston, University of Massachusetts Boston's School for the Environment, Boston Harbor Now, Massachusetts Department of Conservation and Recreation, the National Parks of Boston, and the James M. And Cathleen D. Stone Foundation. The lab is intended to conduct research that brings scientists and community members together to test, design, and monitor nature-based approaches to coastal climate adaptation and restoration, which would directly inform adaptation planning in the Boston area and beyond. While the lab has led shoreline monitoring, a "living seawall" pilot project, and public education and outreach, regulatory hurdles pose a challenge for its larger ambitions to deploy nature-based flood protection in Boston Harbor.

Federal and State Government

Mayors are often lauded as climate heroes, taking bold action to make their cities more sustainable even when policy stagnates at the federal level. But mayors are not autonomous rulers. Under the Dillon Rule, adopted by the US Supreme Court in 1907, municipalities are "political subdivisions of the state," so states have the power to give, change, or take away powers of local governments (*Hunter v. City of Pittsburgh*—207 U.S. 161, 178–79). A city's relationship to state government and to its larger metropolitan region creates important constraints and complexities for mitigating and adapting to climate change. Different states delegate different levels of power to local governments, and many cities are highly constrained in their ability to pursue climate-related policies by their state governments. Cities ultimately depend on state and federal action—as well as driving market forces—to fully transition from fossil fuels to renewable energy.

This is certainly true for Boston, which, like the other cities and towns in Massachusetts, relies on state authority to exercise many municipal decisions and actions. Some of Michelle Wu's proposals for Boston, including abolishing the BPDA and making the MBTA free for riders, rely on legislative actions at the state level, and some proposed climate adaptation projects will require cooperation between adjacent cities and towns. Meanwhile, energy utilities and regional and quasi-state agencies govern much of Boston's energy grid and infrastructure and have differing priorities for the future. Coordination of city and state agencies will pose a challenge to Boston's efforts to update infrastructure, land use, and urban design for greater resiliency. For instance, major roads and areas of parkland are managed by the state Department of Conservation and Recreation, requiring coordination of planning at multiple levels of government.

Massachusetts is a well-resourced state and a clear national leader in climate change policy. But state politics are different from Boston's, and the state's legislation, regulatory administration, and budgetary spending place important constraints on the city's climate goals. Massachusetts has a long tradition of municipal independence. In 1966, after an overwhelming number of special acts of the state legislature that were required to deal with day-to-day matters in cities and towns (Barron et al. 2004), the state passed a home rule amendment to its constitution giving municipalities the right to exercise certain powers through their own legislative bodies (such as Boston's City Council) without the express approval of the state legislature, as long these are not inconsistent with the state's constitution or general laws (Amendment Article 89). But home rule did not create hundreds of autonomous local governments. The state government's limitations on the powers of local governments can foster a sense of caution and constraint in municipal action; as noted in an analysis of home rule policies: "Massachusetts protects home rule in a way that promotes parochialism and frustrates interlocal cooperation rather than in a way that empowers cities and towns to meet the needs of their residents" (Barron et al. 2004, xii).

Politics is an obvious inconsistency between state and city climate governance: at the state level, Democrats dominate the state legislature but in recent history Massachusetts has elected several Republican governors campaigning on low-tax platforms. Republican governors of Massachusetts have taken positions on climate change that lie well left of most of their party, but they have often resisted pressure to enact progressive climate policies. Under Democratic governor Deval Patrick, Massachusetts enacted the landmark Global Warming Solutions Act of 2008, which created a mandate for the state to reduce emissions: 25% below 1990 levels by 2020 and 90% below by 2050. But a 2016 ruling from the Massachusetts Supreme Judicial Court found that the state had failed to fully enforce the law by taking steps to reduce emissions (*Kain v. Dept. of Envtl. Prot.*). Under the Baker-Polito administration, the state achieved its 2020 goals (an estimated 31% emissions reduction) (Commonwealth of Massachusetts, n.d.-b), and that year created a more detailed "decarbonization roadmap" with specific strategies to reach carbon neutrality by 2050 (Ismay et al. 2020). State legislators, meanwhile, pushed to accelerate statewide emissions goals. After lengthy political negotiations between the Governor and state legislature, a new law was passed in 2021, "An Act Creating a Next Generation Roadmap for Massachusetts Climate Policy" (M.G.L. c. 30A, § 4). The law created the first comprehensive and ambitious updates to the 2008 law; made the state's goal of reaching net zero emissions by 2050 enforceable; set incremental emissions goals for meeting those targets; and addressed renewable energy, building codes, environmental justice, and other regulatory changes. That being said, the state's commitments fall short of calls from the UN to accelerate net-zero targets to 2040 (Shankman and Platoff 2023).

Maura Healey, Democratic governor since 2022, established a new position of Climate Chief, who works across executive offices to ensure consistency with state climate goals. The 2021 climate bill requires the state's Executive Office of Energy and Environmental Affairs to set interim emissions limits every five years: the state's Clean Energy and Climate Plan for 2025 and 2040 details strategies to achieve its near-term climate targets. It will require a major increase in electric power across the state while decarbonizing the existing electric grid and improving its efficiency (Commonwealth of Massachusetts 2022a).

Massachusetts' government has engaged in comprehensive adaptation planning since 2011, when it released its first statewide climate adaptation report based on input from an advisory committee consisting of stakeholders from environmental nonprofits, government representatives, and other institutions (Executive Office of Energy and Environmental Affairs and Adaptation Advisory Committee 2011). A 2018 executive order by Republican Governor Charlie Baker called for an "integrated strategy" that included both hazard mitigation and climate adaptation planning, leading to a 2018 State Hazard Mitigation and Climate Adaptation Plan (MA, 2018. A 2022 Massachusetts Climate Change Assessment provided a comprehensive view of climate impacts by region and across social, economic, infrastructural, environmental, and governance sectors (Commonwealth of Massachusetts 2022b). An ongoing ResilientCoasts initiative engages in comprehensive planning for coastal adaptation in the state, led by a new Chief Coastal Resilience Officer housed in the Massachusetts Coastal Zone Management Office (Healey 2023).

Beyond broader policies around emissions targets and adaptation planning, the state's policies in key areas of climate action have consequences for reaching the city's own mitigation and adaptation goals, particularly related to energy infrastructure, building emissions, transportation, and flood control projects. An example of an enabling policy is legislation passed in 1997 allowing community choice aggregation (CCA), an approach to energy procurement that is becoming popular in the United States and is increasingly used to promote green energy (Hsu 2022). Currently, ten states including Massachusetts have adopted legislation that allows for CCA programs in local governments (https://www.leanenergyus.org/cca-by-state). Unlike California's program, which has resulted in several large CCAs that span multiple counties, CCAs in Massachusetts are based on municipality, in keeping with the state's usual town-by-town governing approach (O'Shaughnessy et al. 2019).

An example of a limiting policy is the Massachusetts State Building Code. Under home rule, municipalities can enact their own zoning laws provided they are consistent with state laws, but they cannot adopt building standards that are stricter than the base code (Conservation Law Foundation 2019). For its building energy codes, for instance, Massachusetts adopts the International Energy Conservation Code with some amendments, and regulatory efforts to reduce building emissions in the Boston area have been hampered by requirements not to exceed state codes. In 2009, in response to demand for more efficient standards, the state became the first in the country to establish an optional "stretch code" that focused on building performance, and nearly 300 municipalities in the state adopted it (Commonwealth of Massachusetts, n.d.-a), but represented a modest gain in efficiency. The state Department of Energy Resources (DOER) updated the stretch code after the passage of the 2021 climate bill (Massachusetts Department of Energy Resources 2023). It sets stricter requirements of efficiency in new construction and renovations but falls short of a "net zero" code that many climate advocates had hoped for. It sets new efficiency standards that would greatly help reduce the state's emissions, but allows for continued use of fossil fuels in heating systems (Morgan 2022). The 2021 climate law includes an additional policy of creating a new "net zero" energy code that can help municipalities that opt in take more ambitious steps to promote greener construction beyond what the stretch code achieves. The real estate industry raised concerns that stricter codes will exacerbate an unaffordable housing market, underscoring the need for policies that address decarbonization and affordability together (Bakhshi et al. 2023). State building codes also constrain the abilities of municipalities to require climate change adaptation, particularly because building codes are based on historical climate data. Boston has been able to create technical design guidelines to promote resilience, and more recently, implemented a zoning overlay district that maps to a floodplain with sea-level rise.

Massachusetts runs a consumer-facing initiative called Mass Save, which uses fees on energy bills to offer incentives to residents, institutions, and businesses to improve energy efficiency. The program, which is administered by natural gas and electric utilities, focuses largely on improving cost savings to consumers through energy efficiency measures such as energy audits, home insulation, and efficient appliances, and has helped to improve energy efficiency in homes and residential buildings across Greater Boston. Because utility companies are not required to meet the state's climate goals, however, the program misses opportunities to support more transformative building decarbonization (Hoffer, 2023).

Massachusetts participates in some multi-state energy and climate initiatives. These include the Regional Greenhouse Gas Initiative, the first mandatory market-based emissions reduction initiative in the United States that has been largely effective in promoting emissions reductions across participating states. In 2021, Massachusetts withdrew from the proposed multistate Transportation and Climate Initiative, citing costs burdens, echoing concerns from other cap and trade emissions markets that have failed to fully bear the costs of the programs (Andrew 2008).

In addition to the state regulatory and funding landscape, Boston has faced dramatically shifting priorities and financial support at the federal level that impact its ability to act on climate change. The city has benefitted from recent federal investments, earmarking about $46 million of $559 million received from the American Rescue Plan Act funds passed by Congress in 2021 toward climate resilience and mobility programs. But it has faced cutbacks under both Trump administrations, including the termination of numerous federal grants for energy projects in Massachusetts. Federal grant elimination has paused projects related to climate change and environmental justice. And federal policy changes—including rolling back air quality regulations, rescinding the federal endangerment finding as a basis for regulating greenhouse gas emissions, and removing other environmental standards at the U.S. Environment Protection Agency—could have long-lasting impacts on environmental quality and climate action. More broadly, federal funding cuts and anti-immigration policies have caused a widespread instability and uncertainty in Greater Boston's universities and environmental workforce, which are a critical node in the region's economy.

Given limited federal funding for pre-disaster climate change adaptation in cities, Boston has benefitted from state funding from its Municipal Vulnerability Preparedness grant program, which has helped to support recent planning for extreme heat, the design of a climate-resilient park, and coastal resilience zoning. State funding for climate adaptation has been crucial for other cities and towns in the metropolitan area, many of which lack Boston's dedicated resources and staff to engage in climate change planning. The program funding is modest, with most grants $50,000 or less to engage in planning, with up to $3 million for "action" projects, many of which relate to updating infrastructure. The program originally involved a traditional planning process but created a set of "MVP 2.0" grants in 2023 that focus on greater community involvement in decision-making and addressing root causes of social vulnerability. Massachusetts has taken steps to improve procedural and distributive justice by seeking greater inclusiveness in resilience planning and action.

Metropolitan Governance

Greater Boston's political structure shapes the scale of decision-making across the entire metropolitan system. Many of its municipalities have been working together on climate policies, but larger issues—such as protecting coastlines that cross boundaries—will still be a challenge. The metropolitan area includes the state's wealthiest cities and towns, such as Dover, Weston, Wellesley, and Winchester, as well as cities with the most socially vulnerable residents, including Chelsea, Everett, Malden, Brockton, and Revere. Increases in housing prices in Boston has forced lower-income residents out of the city limits and into other metropolitan cities and suburban towns.

Overcoming competitiveness and parochialism among the many cities and towns that make up Greater Boston is a daunting prospect. Even before climate action was a political priority, municipalities failed to cooperate to address broad regional issues like land use, housing, and transportation. Massachusetts' home rule system works against regional solutions, and the lack of local power may lead municipalities to adopt a strategy of "defensive localism" and avoid getting involved in efforts to address regional problems (Barron et al. 2004). It has stymied efforts to regulate planning in the metro area, leaving smart growth policies, open space protection, affordable housing, and historic preservation to local decision-makers (Hamin et al. 2006).

When considered as a metropolis, Boston's climate challenges become increasingly magnified and complex. While the City of Boston can target its planning and investments in neighborhoods strategically to avoid exacerbating racial and socioeconomic inequities, for instance, there is no mechanism for addressing the wide inequities across cities and towns in Metropolitan Boston, except at a broad state level through environmental justice mandates and other policies to address issues such as housing inequalities. Many of these other municipalities lack the significant budget and resources that Boston has to address issues like climate change impacts and adaptation; for instance, many have had to rely on scientific data from Climate Ready Boston in their own planning, even though the local context of these locations might differ considerably from Boston's (Valdez 2020).

The Metropolitan Area Planning Commission (MAPC) has led several efforts to overcome political fragmentation and engage in regional planning to overcome economic and social challenges in the Boston metro area. Though it has no direct authority over regional government, it helps to shape policy directions in several ways. It leads broad long-range regional planning efforts, focusing on land use strategies to manage growth and policies to promote regional sustainability, climate change resilience, economic equity, affordable housing, health equity, inclusive government, and regional coordination. It provides advisory planning, research, and technical assistance to cities and towns on metropolitan issues, include climate change mitigation and adaptation. MAPC also supports the Metropolitan Mayors Coalition, a group of mayors and managers of 15 cities and towns in the Boston metro area that works on issues that impact the entire region. The group includes a Climate Taskforce to coordinate regional cooperation on climate mitigation and resilience efforts. MAPC also sponsors a Health and Medical Coordinating Coalition across the metro area to help coordinate public health preparedness and emergency responses, though it has no authority over existing municipal systems. With funding from the federal Environmental Protection Agency, MAPC is working with other regional agencies to develop a Greater Boston Climate Action plan, which will create regionwide greenhouse gas emissions inventories and comprehensive climate action planning across the Metropolitan Statistical Area, comprising 167 municipalities in Massachusetts and Southern New Hampshire (Viall 2023). As municipalities recognize a greater need for coordination on climate issues, the MAPC will likely be an increasingly important player in coordinating their actions.

Watershed governance

Chapter 3 raised the challenge of scale when governing climate change and other environmental challenges within urban SETS. Nonprofit organizations devoted to Boston's major river watersheds are an example of governance that crosses municipal boundaries and are providing a path toward metropolitan-scale climate action. Originally developed to address pollution in Boston's major rivers, the Charles River Watershed Association, Mystic River Watershed Association, and the Neponset River Watershed Association, have all added climate resilience to their work, which includes working on cross-boundary issues among multiple cities and towns in their watersheds. Watershed associations and other watershed-based institutions, though limited in funding and authority, can help facilitate collaborative governance of climate issues.

A key example is the Resilient Mystic Collaborative (RMC), which was launched in 2018 with Barr Foundation funding as a collaborative, consensus-based model of climate adaptation in the watershed (Mascarenhas 2020). With a network of leaders from 210 municipalities and several non-municipal public and private stakeholders, the RMC has led research, modeling, planning, and implementation of projects related to flooding, as well as launching Wicked Hot Mystic, a community-based heat mapping project in collaboration with the Museum of Science and Metropolitan Area Planning Council. As an institution that integrates social, environmental, and infrastructural issues across an urban SETS at a watershed scale, RMC is an excellent example of integrated governance of climate risks.

Utilities and Other Agencies

Much of Boston's energy infrastructure and land is owned and managed by state, metropolitan, or quasi-state agencies, posing coordination challenges for climate mitigation, adaptation, and overall system resilience in the city and metropolitan area. Here I focus on four examples of utilities and regional agencies that underscore the complexity of climate transitions that involve multiple levels and layers of governance.

The role of natural gas in the energy transition is an example where utilities, state authorities, environmental activists, and other actors have been misaligned. While committing to a "fossil-free" future, National Grid developed a climate plan that downplays electrification and preserves the continuity of the existing natural gas pipeline system, focusing instead on using alternative fuels such as green hydrogen and "renewable natural gas" (Woerner and Rio 2022). After evaluating the regulatory frameworks for several possible decarbonization pathways for the state, the Massachusetts Department of Public Utilities issued an order rejecting support for renewable natural gas (D.P.U. 20-80-B), making Massachusetts perhaps the first state to require its utilities to decarbonize (Gearino 2023). Clearer regulatory direction from the state will help municipalities seeking to modernize and innovate their energy systems. Boston has so far made only limited advancements in encouraging innovative micro-grids and district energy systems, while utilities and the state lack the capacity and focus to foster innovations at the neighborhood and municipal level (Fitzgerald et al. 2022).

The Massachusetts Water Resources Authority (MWRA) provides the water supply and sewage treatment services to Boston and 60 other communities. Within Boston, the water and sewer systems are managed by the Boston Water and Sewer Commission. Given the historical development of a large and well-protected water supply in Boston, the city does not face critical issues with water pollution or scarcity as many other major cities do. Some communities outside of this system, however, do face future challenges with groundwater changes, increasing drought, and pollution issues exacerbated by climate change (Douglas and Kirshen 2022). Within the Boston metro area, sewage management and water quality are acute challenges, as the MWRA system is designed to release sewage into waterways during storms. While the MWRA has spent $900 million to eliminate combined sewer overflows as part of the Boston Harbor clean-up project, the agency estimates that completely eliminating CSO discharges would cost more than $18 billion on the Charles River alone (MassDEP 2019).

Massport, a quasi-state agency that manages Boston's container port and airport, owns 12.7% of Boston's total land area, making it a key landowner and developer within Boston (its primary revenue is from non-port real estate development on its land), and an important player in the regional climate change response. Massport has launched initiatives to address greenhouse gas emissions in shipping and transportation and created a roadmap for reaching net zero emissions by 2031, ahead of state and federally mandated targets of 2050 (Massport 2022). The plan focuses on upgrading facilities, vehicles, and operations to improve energy efficiency and shift fuel and energy sources toward renewables, but it avoids tackling broader problems like reducing emissions from burning jet fuel (Abel 2022). Massport's climate adaptation response has been mixed. The agency adopted climate resiliency standards for buildings on land it owns, like those issued by the BPDA. While Massport has been at the table in planning processes like Climate Ready Boston, it is described by waterfront stakeholders as focused on protecting its own assets rather than serving as a partner with the city. Given its prominent footprint in Boston, the agency's approach may need to change to accomplish the city's more ambitious goals. Plans to protect the flat, low-lying Seaport District from flooding, for instance, will require Massport's cooperation.

Governance of Boston's public transportation network, overseen by the Massachusetts Bay Transportation Authority (MBTA), has led to an acute crisis in the city that poses major challenges for climate mitigation, social equity, and the ongoing resilience of transportation networks to flooding, heat, and other climate-related impacts. The regional authority was created in 1964 and was subject to underinvestment and periodic changes in governance over the succeeding decades. While the MBTA is critical infrastructure for Boston residents—and an important piece of the city's climate mitigation strategies—the city has lacked representation in its decision-making. The state's budget for 2023 allows the City of Boston to appoint a member of the MBTA's board of directors for the first time, giving the city greater influence in agency decisions.

Chapter 6

OPPORTUNITIES AND CHALLENGES: MITIGATION, ADAPTATION, EQUITY

In its climate action to date, Boston has pursued the five "pathways to urban transformation" described in ARC 3.2 that were mentioned in this book's Introduction. It is engaging in both climate adaptation and mitigation efforts, sometimes in a siloed fashion but increasingly integrated, making use of local technical and scientific expertise to produce robust knowledge about its carbon footprint and potential future impacts of climate change. It has brought disaster risk reduction and climate adaptation into urban development in through concrete policies. It has engaged residents and a variety of stakeholders in climate planning. It has worked to embed equity and justice into its plans and policies. And it has participated in national and transnational networks and explored financing tools to improve its adaptive capacity, in addition to directing municipal spending to climate related staff and initiatives.

But the city faces numerous challenges to meeting its goals of becoming carbon neutral and adapting to growing climate risks in a way that is socially equitable. Challenges include path dependencies in the city's infrastructure and its governance systems, a lack of for support from higher levels of government, and social backlash against climate policies that may stymie some policy efforts. This chapter explores some of the city's specific opportunities and challenges around three areas of climate action: mitigation (specifically energy, buildings, transportation, and waste), adaptation (focusing on threats of sea-level rise and coastal storms, stormwater flooding, and extreme heat), and social equity.

Energy

Much of Boston's progress on reducing its emissions will not stem from municipal policy at all, but from future greening of New England's electric grid (Cleveland et al. 2019). That will depend upon progress on building the capacity for renewable energy in the state and New England region, which is subject to economic and political advances and impediments. Currently over half of the state's electricity comes from natural gas, and the other half largely includes a mix of nuclear power; hydroelectric power; and wind, solar, and waste-to-power systems. As part of an effort to green its energy grid, Massachusetts has set clean energy requirements for retail sellers of electricity that increase over time, reaching a target of 80% low- or no-greenhouse gas emitting electricity by 2050 (310 CMR 7.75). This transition will require significant new investments in clean energy infrastructure, including hydropower, wind, and solar energy. A key piece of the state's overall clean energy plan, for instance, relies on hydropower from Quebec, a project that has faced legal battles with opponents in Maine, which the transmission line would pass through, and funding uncertainties from Massachusetts lawmakers (Mohl 2023). The state is also counting on tapping into its vast potential for offshore wind energy and has set an ambitious goal is of producing 5,600 megawatts of wind power by 2027, a goal that would require vastly expanding its clean energy workforce (Massachusetts Clean Energy Center 2023). But this expansion is currently uncertain without federal support for renewable energy under the Trump administration.

Massachusetts has a detailed plan for achieving net zero emissions by 2050; an analysis from the MA Executive Office of Energy and Environmental Affairs found that the state has feasible paths to achieve net-zero emissions by 2050 while maintaining a "healthy, equitable, and thriving economy," given federal and regional cooperation (Ismay et al. 2020). The role of natural gas in the state's energy transition is highly debated. Over half of Massachusetts households use natural gas for heating, while 20% use electricity and fuel oil, respectively. As part of a state-led process investigating the "future of gas," the state's five gas utilities advanced visions of using biomethane and hydrogen as cleaner fuel alternatives with existing gas pipelines. But that vision was countered by strong grassroots activism against the continued use of natural gas. The state Department of Public Utilities ultimately ruled in 2023 that the state should move away from natural gas, making it the first state to create such an order, which laid out a framework for transitioning away from gas.

Massachusetts is also participating in an innovative new approach to turning gas utilities into providers of gas-free networked geothermal systems. Eversource became the first public utility to launch a pilot networked geothermal system, which uses ground-source heat pumps linked by an underground pipe network to efficiently heat and cool neighborhoods. The project, piloted in Framingham, Massachusetts, could serve as model for other communities in the Boston metro area.

Some cities within the metro area that have taken aggressive and creative approaches to climate mitigation, including Cambridge, Somerville, and Newton. The state's strong climate action planning has helped enable climate action at the municipal level, but regulatory hurdles and bureaucracy at the state level have also hindered municipal clean energy and energy equity programs. The Department of Public Utilities, for instance, has been critiqued for putting regulatory roadblocks in the path of programs like an effort to bring solar credits to low-income residents in Boston (Shankman 2021).

Within Boston, the city has taken steps toward promoting renewable energy, including creating a community choice aggregation (CCA) program (see including creating the community choice aggregation (CCA) program described in Chapter 5), which uses aggregated purchasing power to lower energy costs and provide greener energy to residents. The city created the Community Choice Electricity program in 2021; residents are automatically enrolled in a default plan that includes some renewable energy but can opt into a plan that includes up to 100% renewable energy. As the program matures, the city has an opportunity to increase participation in the fully renewable option, particularly as renewable energy becomes more available and cost-effective statewide. Meanwhile, continued energy efficiency—including strategies to reduce energy use in buildings described in the next section—will greatly moderate the increase in Boston's electricity demand in the future, even as the city grows in population and electrifies much of its buildings and transportation (Cleveland et al. 2019).

Boston has seen a significant increase in rooftop solar installation aided by state policies including net metering. But these installations represent only a small part of the city's estimated potential, and Boston has not ranked in the top tier of cities for solar installation (Environment Massachusetts Research & Policy Center 2018). To improve its use of renewable energy, the city will need to take better advantage of rooftop solar across the city and metropolitan area, make rooftop solar a possibility for more rental units and low-income households, and modernize aspects of its energy grid (Fitzgerald et al. 2022). The city is also looking to take advantage of its widespread district energy systems, including six systems providing energy-efficient steam-based thermal energy to universities, hospitals, and other institutions throughout Boston and Cambridge. These systems normally rely on nonrenewable fuels, but Vicinity Energy, which operates a large district energy system servicing 70 million square feet of space in Boston and Cambridge, has issued a plan to electrify its energy systems (Vicinity Energy 2021).

Buildings

Boston's buildings represent one of the city's greatest challenges, both in terms of mitigating the city's greenhouse gas emissions and adapting to the impacts of climate change. The city has experienced an unprecedented growth in development over the past decade, and it is planning for continued growth (City of Boston 2017a). Boston's policy evolution in this area is useful example that other cities can learn from. Overall, it demonstrates a trajectory from largely voluntary and opportunistic strategies toward formal regulation of buildings. Becoming carbon-neutral would require not only greening the city's energy grid and improving energy efficiency but eliminating fossil fuel use in buildings through widespread electrification, including heating and hot water systems.

Large buildings (over 50,000 square feet) account for an estimated 60% of Boston's building emissions (42% of the city's total), and Boston has led the nation in developing policy tools to address energy use in larger buildings. It was the first U.S. city to create a green building standard in its zoning laws in 2007 during the Menino administration. An executive order set a LEED Silver standard for new municipal buildings, and the Boston Redevelopment Authority implemented an amendment to the city's building code (Article 37) to promote green building in new large non-municipal buildings (over 50,000 square feet) through adoption of LEED certification. But the amendment only required that buildings be "LEED Certifiable under the most appropriate LEED building rating system" (Article 37-4) but did not actually require them to obtain LEED certification, which limited impact of the law (Beauregard et al. 2014). LEED benchmarking can be viewed as one of a collection of "governance alternatives" that have been popular policy choices for municipalities striving to advance climate action without broader state and federal government action, but which often make only marginal improvements in urban emissions (van der Heijden 2021b). Such policies often seek to achieve ambitious climate targets without the ability to implement mandates through building codes and legislation. The LEED certification system has endured numerous critiques over the years (Amiri et al. 2019), particularly for serving as marketing tool for development rather than reducing greenhouse gas emissions (Dilworth and Stokes 2013). In Boston, the use of green buildings figured prominently in press and advertising for real estate in the city, such as in the massive Seaport Square development (Boston Redevelopment Authority 2010).

Based on recommendations in Boston's 2011 Climate Action Plan, in 2013, the city adopted a new ordinance, the Building Energy Reporting and Disclosure Ordinance (BERDO), requiring large buildings (buildings over 35,000 square feet, or residential buildings that have 35 units or more, or parcels that have buildings totaling 100,000 square feet or 100 units) to report their annual energy and water use. Though the ordinance created a reporting tool rather than a mandate, city data shows that in the first four years of BERDO, large commercial buildings lowered their total energy use by more than 7% (Cleveland et al. 2019). But while BERDO helped to raise awareness of building emissions and likely had some impact, it had significant limitations. Compliance in reporting reached a high of 90% in 2017 but dropped down to 84% by 2020, and less than two-thirds of covered buildings have completed a required energy assessment (City of Boston Environment Department 2021). The city gradually worked to enact more stringent standards of building performance for municipal buildings. In 2019, Mayor Walsh issued an executive order that set a net zero standard for municipal buildings (Walsh 2019).

After relying on largely incremental and non-regulatory strategies to green non-municipal buildings, in 2021, Boston adopted a new version of the citywide building ordinance, called BERDO 2.0, one of the strongest policies in the country to curb emissions from buildings and one of the first to set a citywide building performance standard. Owners of large buildings (20,000 square feet or more for commercial buildings, 15 units or more for residential buildings) must report energy and water use each year and must progressively reduce their emissions to meet a net zero standard by 2050. One of the other notable advances in BERDO 2.0 is the role of community involvement. The first iteration of BERDO was largely a technical requirement that did little to involve the community or disseminate reported data. BERDO 2.0 made significant strides to involve the community, creating a Community Advisory Group that focused on policies that help residents heat and cool their homes more efficiently, improve air quality, and create jobs while avoiding exacerbating displacement of current residents (Barkdoll 2021).

Boston's efforts to improve energy efficiency in buildings have sometimes been constrained by requirements that municipalities are not allowed to exceed the state's energy codes. The state has issued "stretch" energy codes that municipalities can opt into, which allow for better energy efficiency in new construction. The passage of the state's landmark climate bill in 2021 offered new ways for municipalities to reduce emissions by creating a Specialized Stretch Code that promotes net-zero buildings, which Boston and many other municipalities in its metro area have adopted. The code does not ban fossil fuel use but requires that large multifamily housing complexes built in the city must achieve Passive House certification, as well as meeting one of three efficiency pathways (zero energy, all electric, or mix-fuel with certain efficiency measures). Boston was not successful, however, in becoming one of ten municipalities enrolling in a state pilot program to fully ban fossil fuels from new construction and major renovations, which included nearby municipalities Brookline, Newton, and Cambridge.

In 2025, Boston became the first city in the United States to add a requirement to its zoning code that major new buildings (20,000 feet or more) achieve net zero emissions. It also now asks buildings going through its Article 80 development review process to report on the embodied carbon of the building's construction and to conduct a life cycle assessment of its emissions.

Boston's policy evolution around buildings provides an example of a city moving over the course of nearly two decades from opportunistic, voluntary, and negotiated approaches to promoting green building to a stricter regulatory approach and more ambitious targets. It provides a model for other cities for harnessing regulation to improve the city's building-related energy emissions. But its achievements have been made through regulatory obstacles at the state level and challenge from within the real estate industry, which Boston depends heavily on for its revenue and economic growth and has lobbied against recent efforts to ban fossil fuels in buildings. Boston's gradual evolution on building emissions unfolded at a time of unprecedented growth. The city created a new neighborhood of large buildings in the Seaport District, and it added 4–6 million square feet of built space each year from 2014 to 2021 (City of Boston 2019). While Boston implemented green building policies in this time, it also created many buildings that do not meet the standards needed for a carbon-free future. Post-pandemic, new development has slowed in the city just at the time that more stringent regulations are in place. While the city has led on policies to regulate building emissions, it has also missed opportunities to cultivate a more energy-efficient built environment.

The next challenge and opportunity for Boston lies in reducing emissions in the city's vast stock of older buildings. Electrification of small buildings will be necessary for the city to achieve a more "durable reduction" in emissions, rather than resorting to pursuing renewable energy credits to achieve emissions goals (Fitzgerald et al. 2022, 41). Residential buildings represent about half of building-related emissions, and Boston still has a high number of residences using fuel oil for heating, although that number has dropped by more than half in recent years (City of Boston 2019). As many residences have recently switched to natural gas heating, a widespread shift to electrification would require a multipronged effort to incentivize homeowners and landlords. Retrofits have been discussed in Boston's planning documents, and the city recently launched a grant program supported by federal American Rescue Plan Act (ARPA) dollars to offset the cost of energy retrofits in housing developments with significant numbers of affordable units, as well as a Healthy and Green Retrofit Pilot Program to encourage existing buildings to achieve net zero standards. REALIZE-MA, a program led by the Rocky Mountain Institute (RMI), works directly with contractors, architects, and engineers in the state to develop deep energy retrofits in affordable housing projects (King and Jemtrud 2025). While Boston could learn from recent government-led experiments such as New York State Energy Research &

Development Authority's RetrofitNY program, a recent analysis from the Boston Foundation argues that Boston's private philanthropy sector should provide financing to scale up building retrofits (Ellison 2024).

Transportation

Transportation emissions represent 30% of Boston's total emissions, according to the city's emissions data. As with energy systems, municipalities like Boston are constrained in what they can do to achieve emissions targets for the transportation sector. Much of Boston's emissions reductions to date comes from federal and state regulations that improve fuel efficiency of vehicles, over which cities have little control (City of Boston 2011). But cities can enact policies to improve efficiency in municipal vehicles, make it easier for residents to adopt electric vehicles, and reduce vehicle-miles traveled through a wide variety of policies and infrastructure investments that discourage car use and promote public transportation, walkability, and bikeability. Boston has implemented policies to address transportation-related emissions under direct control of the city, including municipal vehicles and school buses (City of Boston Environment Department 2021). But the city faces challenges in transportation investment and political opposition that complicate its transition toward sustainability.

Boston created a comprehensive transportation plan in 2017 called Go Boston 2030. A 2020 analysis of the City's progress on the plan, conducted by the non-profit LivableStreets Alliance, found that the city is on track or making progress on most of its targets, but has fallen behind on others (Gag 2020). The city has improved safety and access within specific intersections and transportation corridors, but it has avoided adopting more aggressive policies that discourage driving and parking in the city, such as congestion pricing.

Like many other U.S. cities, Boston's planning over the past decade has been shaped by the Complete Streets movement, which centers the rights and perspectives of non-car users of roads (Zehngebot and Peiser 2014). Over half of city-owned land lies in public rights of way, representing a vast territory that could be put to better use to achieve several municipal goals, from emissions reductions to heat island mitigation to stormwater absorption. Along with San Francisco and New York City, Boston has been noted for its comprehensive embrace of the Complete Streets approach; the City of Boston initiated a Complete Streets program in 2009 and issued a set of detailed and highly illustrative design guidelines for street design and construction that allow more room for multimodal transit. Boston has implemented policies to address transportation-related emissions under direct control of the city, including a Diesel Emissions Reduction Ordinance in 2015 that places emissions standards on City of Boston owned and operated vehicles, and efforts to reduce emissions across its fleet of school buses (City of Boston Environment Department 2021).

One of the challenges is persistent car dependency. While known as a relatively dense, walkable city, particularly in its compact downtown core, many Bostonians are far more car-dependent than the city's reputation might suggest. Parking, for instance, is often at the crux of neighborhood debates over new housing developments. Residents frequently resist projects that don't provide on-site parking because of increased competition for limited on-street parking spots and increased traffic from residents seeking parking in nearby areas. Boston has seen an increase in automobile dependence and traffic congestion, propelled by population growth. Residents of Boston have not been rushing to stop using their cars, evidenced by an overall growth in households with two or more cars and little growth in car-free households (Basu and Ferreira 2021). Boston consistently ranks as the top one or two "most congested" cities in the United States by consulting firm INRIX. The sudden advent of ride-hailing services like Uber and Lyft initially promised to reduce car ownership but analyses indicate that ride-hailing services likely contribute to growing emissions by adding new cars and discouraging other forms of transport (MAPC 2019).

Like many cities, Boston experienced a dramatic drop in transit ridership during the COVID-19 pandemic, with transit ridership falling to 75% of expected levels during the pandemic's first year (Basu and Ferreira 2021). The issue was compounded during the pandemic by a growing safety and reliability crisis with the MBTA. The system faces a backlog of needed repairs and upgrades, delays and problems related to new subway cars, stations that are literally crumbling. widespread staffing shortages, frequently delayed schedules, disabled trains, and, even more alarmingly, several shocking safety lapses that have caused injuries and deaths to riders. A federal inquiry and safety report identified several failings by the MBTA to prioritize safety in day-to-day operations, which it must fix to receive continued federal support (Federal Transit Administration 2022). Subway ridership is still only 50-60% of pre-pandemic levels, according to city data.

The MBTA represents a generational challenge for a city that had the distinction of opening the nation's first subway tunnel in 1897. Parts of the aging system have not seen upgrades for decades. Frequent service interruptions for these long-neglected repairs further discourage ridership. Transit represents a mismatch between the scale of urban problems and the scale of decision-making within urban SETS. The city is dependent on state-level investments and on the management decisions of the MBTA to achieve its transportation emissions goals, and the current situation is a consequence of longstanding political disagreements over MBTA funding at the state level. In 2023, the City of Boston was given a seat on the MBTA Board of Directors for the first time, reflecting the historic lack of representation from the city.

Given the challenges of changing entrenched car-centric transportation patterns, Boston has made important progress in promoting a shift to electric vehicles. A Zero-Emission Vehicle Roadmap supported by Bloomberg Philanthropies' American Cities Climate Challenge lays out policies to boost the city's modest levels of electric vehicle ownership and to fully electrify the city's own fleet of vehicles (City of Boston 2020). The city, for instance, is working to ensure more equitable access to electric vehicle chargers, which are currently clustered in downtown neighborhoods (Moura 2023). Legislation has been proposed at the state level to examine congestion pricing, which could help shift demand toward lower-carbon modes of travel (Curwin 2023). In sum, Boston has enacted comprehensive and thoughtful plans for reducing transportation-related emissions, but it has focused on incentive-based programs and targeted improvements to urban design. Reaching the city's emissions goals will depend on aligning municipal actions with higher-level government regulation and investment, as well as market shifts in electric vehicles.

Boston has often been viewed as an unsafe city for bicycling, though the city has been taking efforts over the past decade or so to improve its bicycle infrastructure. The larger challenge is a social one: Boston, like many cities around the world, faces significant opposition to efforts to change its car-centric streets. The city's investments have increase bicycle ridership and Boston now has an extensive bike share network, an e-bike incentive program, and a cargo bike incentive program for delivery drivers. Still, Bostonians have not shifted heavily toward using bicycles for commuting to work instead of cars, and the city has fallen behind some of its own targets for improvements and (Gag 2020). Boston has experienced 'bikelash' (Wild et al. 2018) against bike lanes in some neighborhoods, forcing the Wu administration to scale back its plans to expand bike infrastructure. Rhetoric against sustainable transportation infrastructure bike lanes has come from multiple perspectives; in the neighborhood of Mattapan, for instance, communities of color have linked bike lanes to ongoing processes of gentrification and displacement. In Boston and other nearby communities, such as Cambridge, infrastructure for increasing bicycle ridership has prompted backlash from small businesses. Moreover, bike lanes became a major point of political attack in the 2025 mayoral race.

Boston's experience highlights broader tensions in many cities around green gentrification and the right to the sustainable city, underscoring how sustainability efforts must consider underlying power dynamics within the city (Gould and Lewis 2016). Alignments between sustainability and other social goals such as equity, justice, and economic development are complex and contested. Efforts to redesign streets with dedicated bus lanes in Boston have also faced pushback because of their perceived impact on small businesses and the parking needs of residents. These are social debates, but they also reflect an infrastructural challenge of altering Boston's constrained historic street network to accommodate a growing population and multiple uses, which includes the intensifying use of delivery trucks and rideshare vehicles. Implementing coherent transportation policy across the metropolitan area is also challenging; someone biking to work from Boston to Cambridge or from Chelsea to East Boston may only travel a short distance but encounter very different levels of infrastructure to support safe bicycling or electric vehicle charging. State-level planning and metropolitan cooperation through the MAPC Metro Mayors paths for achieving greater cooperation on transportation-related policy and other issues.

Waste

Waste accounts for just a fraction of a percentage of Boston's total emissions, but it is a major policy focus for a city seeking to become sustainable and carbon neutral. Boston has taken several e steps to manage its waste streams and reduce emissions. With input from a Zero Waste Advisory Committee, Boston has adopted a Zero Waste Plan with a goal of becoming a zero-waste community and boosting its recycling rate to 80% from about 25% (Cook et al. 2019). The city has had a plastic bag ordinance since 2018, which bans most stores from providing single-use handled plastic bags and to charge customers for handled bags. Boston has launched a program to provide technical assistance for reuse, recycling, and salvage of construction materials to reduce construction waste. The city collects and composts leaf and yard waste and Christmas trees and makes compost available to community. Following a change in statewide ban on textile disposal in 2022, the city launched a curbside textile recycling program and a curbside food waste collection service. Boston has also invested in programs to encourage reuse of building materials and repair of consumer goods. But Boston has not adopted urban metabolism-based planning frameworks or "circular city" programs that have been adopted in Seattle, WA, and other cities outside the United States. As noted in the Introduction, the city does not explicitly measure and work to reduce consumption-related emissions. An important aspect of Boston's waste metabolism is its impact on environmental equity across Greater Boston. Most of the city's waste is brought to an incinerator and landfill in nearby Saugus, which lies near an ecologically sensitive salt marsh and a low-income environmental justice community; this impact outside the city's borders is not explicitly addressed in its waste planning.

Sea-Level Rise and Coastal Storms

Maps and graphics depicting flooded neighborhoods from future sea-level rise have received a great deal of media attention and policy discussion in Boston. These projections have gained urgency with coastal storms, including major winter storm flooding in 2018, and a growing number of areas of the city that are frequently flooded by astronomical high tides. The City of Boston produces a Natural Hazard Mitigation Plan—a requirement for hazard mitigation funding from the Federal Emergency Management Agency (FEMA)—that includes 34 priority actions across the city that include broad strategies such as promoting resilient design and green infrastructure to specific projects such as fixing roads prone to flooding (City of Boston 2021).

Municipal governments play a critical role in climate change adaptation, as it is at the local level that many decisions about relevant factors like land use and development, emergency response, and water resources are made (Nordgren et al. 2016). Boston has been a leader in incorporating resilient design for sea-level rise and storms into its considerable new development. After several years of encouraging ad hoc solutions in flood-prone areas, in 2017, the BPDA adopted a Resiliency Policy requiring developers of major building projects to consider the impacts of future climate conditions (Boston Planning & Development Agency 2017). Two years later, the BPDA adopted a set of Coastal Flood Resilience Design Guidelines, that present a detailed "resilience toolkit" of best practices for flood-proofing measures in various building types (Boston Planning and Development Agency 2019). The checklist has been influential for other U.S. coastal cities facing threats of sea-level rise, and the BPDA's Guidelines have received national recognition (American Planning Association 2020). But the checklist itself does not set out requirements, and it is generally used as an entry point into negotiations in the BPDA's Project Review process.

Following recommendations from Climate Ready Boston to incorporate resilience directly into zoning (City of Boston 2016), the city created a Coastal Flood Resilience Overlay District (Boston Zoning Code, Article 25A), which requires projects undergoing resilience review with the BPDA to comply with its Coastal Flood Resilience Design Principles based on the projected 1% chance flood plain with 40 inches of sea-level rise. Paralleling the city's evolution on building energy standards from a voluntary energy reporting system (BERDO) to a mandated emissions standard (BERDO 2.0), the creation of an overlay district formalizes previously voluntary measures into municipal law, making the city's approach to resilience construction more robust. The city also adopted its first Wetlands Ordinance, which will help protect natural resources and allow for new standards for development in floodplain areas.

Through its resiliency checklist and zoning, Boston has focused on setting specific and quantitative standards for buildings in current and future flood zones. The City of Cambridge has also adopted flood resilience standards into its zoning code as of 2023, based on sea-level rise projections for 2070 (Ordinance No. 2022-9 Section 22.80). Boston's approach of developing detailed requirements for waterfront buildings has helped to create a new level of flood proofing standards in new construction. But it may have tradeoffs: in analyzing the impacts of Boston's regulatory approach, for instance, Markus and Savini (2016) found that developers in the South Boston Waterfront area quickly responded to Boston's resilience regulations by "complying to basic standards without attempting any experiment" (2016, 511). While Boston has enacted policies to promote flood-proofing and building-level resilience, it has also enacted policies that may increase exposure and vulnerability by encouraging new development in floodplains (Woodruff et al. 2021).

Ultimately, Boston will need much more than resilient buildings to protect its vulnerable neighborhoods from flooding; it is clear protecting waterfront neighborhoods would require more extensive district-level flood protection systems. Through the Climate Ready Boston initiative, the city has developed a clear plan to protect its 47 miles of shoreline at sea levels expected later in the century, focusing on low-lying areas and key flood pathways. Yet for all its planning for climate adaptation along its shoreline, Boston has not yet identified large-scale investments to turn these plans into reality. Most adaptation projects that have been completed along the shoreline have involved parcel-by-parcel protection measures. Stitching together larger flood protection for areas with a mix of public and private landowners will be challenging. Enacting what the city has called "district-scale solutions" will require coordinated planning and marshaling new sources of financial support (Kruel et al. 2018; Levy 2018).

An ongoing debate in Boston and its metropolitan region is the scale at which such solutions should be constructed. A 2018 study from a team led by the University of Massachusetts Boston and funded by the Barr Foundation investigated the possibility of creating a massive Harbor-wide barrier system, which would include a storm-surge gate. A barrier solution would require planning, designing, constructing, and maintaining a large and structurally complex flood control system offshore in Boston Harbor, and would be capital-intensive, likely costing tens of billions of dollars for construction and maintenance (Kirshen 2018). A harbor barrier, however, would protect large areas with one intervention, providing an equitable solution that does not place better protection in one neighborhood over another, and it could potentially include newly activated green spaces along the barrier in connection with the Harbor Islands. One of the biggest disadvantages of a flood-gate solution is that it does not mitigate against sea-level rise, only storm surges. Given that many areas of the city will be directly threatened with regular tidal flooding with sea-level rise, shoreline interventions would still be required.

The UMass Boston study reinforced the path that the city had already pursued with Climate Ready Boston, and it informed continued planning strategies focused on shore-based protection. But this decision is still contested. A stakeholder group led by former State Senator William Golden has argued that a "layered defense system" that includes sea gates should continue to be explored, particularly given that the UMass Boston study only examined a limited set of possibilities for offshore flood protection (Golden 2021). These debates parallel discussions in the New York City area, which pursued numerous shore-based plans after Hurricane Sandy, while the U.S. Army Corps of Engineers (USACE) has proposed installing a dozen storm surge gates protecting New York Harbor, an intervention that may have significant environmental impacts.

While Boston has been working to harness private development to improve resiliency, larger-scale solutions would almost certainly require major federal investment. The USACE launched a multiyear study of coastal resilience in Boston in 2022, in partnership with the City of Boston. The process of conducting the study will involve a public participation process that could help refine and coalesce the various visions of Boston's shoreline into implementable plans. While the Corps is most known for large and complicated flood solutions like dams and levees, the agency has been undergoing a shift toward nature-based strategies; the study in Boston will consider options such as using salt marshes, living levees, tiered green spaces, as well as vertical flood walls. It will also consider longer-term land use planning and the possibility of planning ahead for managed retreat in some areas.

With the luxury of engaging in multiyear planning ahead of a disastrous storm, Boston has not only developed a set of specific strategies to protect vulnerable neighborhoods but has engaged numerous stakeholders in the process. The city's new Office for Climate Resilience is anticipated to better coordinate these kinds of projects, and the city's new Planning Department includes a Coastal Resilience Delivery Team to identify and implement projects. Boston's efforts to create municipal capacity and consensus networks through its climate change planning will likely provide a key advantage in implementing adaptation measures using federal and state dollars. But it does not fully address the yawning gaps in funding between what the city has planned and what it can finance. Furthermore, the long process of public engagement in resilience planning threatens to create public confusion and exhaustion as communities are drawn into plans that are never implemented. An example is a long-term planning process for Moakley Park, a large public park in South Boston, which was launched in 2018 and garnered attention for its innovative, resilience landscape, but remained without clear funding or implementation plans for several years (Fitzgerald et al. 2022) and is currently in an uncertain position due to Trump Administration's cancellation of the Building Resilient Infrastructure and Communities (BRIC) grant program, which would have provided $23 million to the project.

Numerous stakeholders involved in Boston's waterfront have expressed interest in flood protection that also creates a greener shoreline and provide so-called "co-benefits" such as recreation, open space, and ecosystem improvements. Such projects have the promise of integrating infrastructural needs with social and ecological benefits. But the Boston Harbor shoreline is highly developed, posing challenges for creating nature-based flood protection within existing hardened shorelines. Shifting waterfront land to green space and restoring intertidal features to previously hardened shorelines could run counter to existing patterns of development that rely on the revenue generated by waterfront redevelopment (Shi 2020). Already, however, projects are being proposed or developed that transform former waterfront piers in East Boston and Charlestown to parkland rather than private development, incorporating natural marine habitat into the designs.

Looming over these citywide planning efforts for shoreline protection is the question of how to coordinate adaptation measures across the city and metropolitan area. Climate Ready Boston's strategies will require changes in federal, state, and local regulations and regulatory processes (Kruel et al. 2018). More coordination is necessary across agencies to protect Boston's regional infrastructure from the impacts of climate change, including parts of the MBTA such as the highly vulnerable Blue Line, Boston's Central Artery Tunnel, and large areas of low-lying coastal land in Boston owned by Massport. These agencies typically engage in their own climate resiliency planning that may differ from the city's. Other coastal adaptation issues cross municipal boundaries and may require metropolitan coordination. For example, the region's major food distribution center lies the city of Everett in an area highly vulnerable to flooding (Commonwealth of Massachusetts 2022b).

The city and its metro region currently lack clear governance structures for planning and executing regional flood protection. Boston's climate action plan calls for establishing an Infrastructure Coordination Committee that allows municipalities across the metropolitan area to improve infrastructure resiliency together (City of Boston 2019). So far, however, the MAPC's

Metro-Mayors Resiliency Taskforce is the only formal body to engage in this type of planning. Numerous stakeholders have begun to call for a regional authority, akin to the Massachusetts Water Resources Authority, to oversee the planning and implementation of coastal resilience projects in the state (Fitzgerald and Wormser 2023). Such an authority would have the ability to marshal federal funding and spearhead regulatory changes to facilitate widespread coastal adaptation, but it could have tradeoffs over the current municipal-led approach.

Climate-vulnerable areas of the city are simultaneously facing exorbitant housing costs within one of the country's most expensive housing and rental markets. Boston faces a series of tensions and tradeoffs related to housing and climate risk. Many of Boston's policies seek to increase housing—and particularly affordable housing—by encouraging development in underdeveloped areas of the city at high risk of flooding, an approach that could ultimately increase exposure to flooding across the city (Woodruff et al. 2021). Boston and its neighboring coastal communities in Boston Harbor face a significant loss of property tax revenue from coastal flooding later in the century, which will create challenges for investing in coastal resilience, particularly in communities that lack financial resources to fund privately funded adaptation (Commonwealth of Massachusetts 2022b).

Stormwater Flooding

While coastal flooding with sea-level rise has been the focus of a great deal of planning and policy creation in Boston, the broader risk of inland flooding in many parts of the metropolitan area has not been fully addressed. Inland flooding from extreme precipitation events is expected to worsen in Greater Boston. Stormwater is the major source of excess nutrients and other pollutants to Boston's waterways, particularly its rivers that suffer from water quality problems and seasonal algae blooms. The Boston Water and Sewer Commission, which oversees the sewer and stormwater has often taken a lead in modeling and mapping stormwater flooding. The agency has commissioned its own analyses and proposed coastal flood solutions for areas like Fort Point Channel that contradict the city's own resiliency plans (Chesto 2023), an indication of conflicting approaches to coastal resilience across agencies.

Some critics have argued that stormwater is overlooked in the City of Boston's resilience planning (pointing, for instance, to large areas of hardscape that was permitted in the Seaport District and other recent developments). The city created initial stormwater flood maps as part of Climate Ready Boston, but these maps have not been updated with more rigorous data. The Wu administration has hired a cabinet-level Director of Green Infrastructure to lead an integrated model of green infrastructure that coordinates collaboration on projects across city agencies. The city also created a green infrastructure policy with standards for municipal projects (City of Boston 2022c). Boston is piloting a project to incorporate green infrastructure into curb bump-outs on its streets and is offering training for small-scale green infrastructure projects. So far, however, new green space and green infrastructure projects in Boston have largely followed overall trajectories of real estate development (City of Boston 2023), making the city highly reliant on private investment for these kinds of projects. BWSC has expanded its stormwater program and implemented a stormwater fee system in 2024.

Stormwater pollution and flooding are a regional concern across the metropolitan area that requires cross-boundary cooperation and planning. Cities and towns have been engaged in long-term efforts to control stormwater pollution to the rivers in the Boston metro area in coordination with the Environmental Protection Agency. The region's watershed associations for the Neponset, Charles, and Mystic rivers have taken key leadership roles in this work. New EPA standards under a Clean Water Act permit require major reductions in nutrient loads from 34 municipalities along the Charles River. Meeting these requirements will involve investing more in green infrastructure in both new and existing development (Moraff 2023). Increasingly, watershed institutions have included climate resiliency and flood control strategies in their work. The MAPC has also coordinated regional planning around stormwater, including disseminating resources to cities and towns such as a low-impact development toolkit and regulatory language for resilient land use planning. Across the metropolitan area, more will need to be done to prepare residents for increased flood risks. An MAPC study found that a major inland flood event in 2010 left widespread flooding throughout Greater Boston, and most disaster claims came from areas outside of federal flood hazard areas where residents were unaware of possible flood risks (Metropolitan Area Planning Council 2023).

Extreme Heat

For many years, extreme heat was a lower priority in city planning than sea-level rise, which was the focus of a highly public Climate Ready Boston planning process in several waterfront neighborhoods. There are reasons for this omission: ask a Bostonian about climate change, and you might hear the opinion that warmer winters are a welcome side effect in New England. Bostonians overall have been less threatened by rising temperatures than many other parts of the United States. But recent summer heat waves have taken a toll on residents, particularly in dense neighborhoods where many residents lack air conditioning (Selig 2022). Heat waves have also impacted the city's infrastructure, including subway track buckling and heat-related speed restrictions (City of Boston 2022b).

Although extreme heat has been recognized as a threat to Boston, it was arguably overlooked by planners for several years. In spite of the unevenness of Boston's heat island, for instance, Climate Ready Boston emphasized heat as a threat that was "spread across the city" rather than requiring a localized focused (City of Boston 2016, xxxix). Consequently, it advocated for citywide solutions for extreme heat but targeted solutions for sea-level rise. The 2016 report focused on eight neighborhoods—seven of which were coastal neighborhoods facing flooding risks, and one (Roxbury) that faced multiple vulnerabilities of flooding and extreme heat. Subsequent Climate Ready Boston neighborhood planning efforts focused exclusively on coastal resilience in five neighborhoods (consolidating study areas in East Boston and Charlestown) and did not include Roxbury.

It was not until 2022 that Boston released a heat plan, Heat Resilience Solutions for Boston, which remedied this oversight with a comprehensive analysis of heat vulnerability in Boston. The plan is based on updated science: modeled air temperature maps that capture urban heat index (UHI) and identify areas that remain hotter longer and remain hot at night (City of Boston 2022b). The plan also took an approach it described as "centering environmental justice and equity in heat resilience" (City of Boston 2022b, 88). Rather than approach heat as a citywide problem, it characterized heat vulnerability as deeply unequal, with extreme heat impacts disproportionately burdening some communities over others and focused on neighborhoods with high extreme temperatures as environmental justice populations: Chinatown, Dorchester, East Boston, Mattapan, and Roxbury. It grapples with Boston's history of racist land use policies by including an analysis comparing heat in areas historically shaped by redlining with other neighborhoods.

The plan includes 26 proposed strategies for alleviating heat risk in Boston, including short-term and long-term actions and an implementation timeline. Short-term strategies include enhancing Boston's network of cooling centers and piloting outdoor cooling during heat waves. Longer-term strategies include changing Boston's built environment to minimize urban heat, such as creating a cool roofs program modeled on a successful program in New York City, and expanding the urban tree canopy, parks, open space, and other green infrastructure. The plan also includes updating the BPDA's resiliency checklist and guidelines to incorporate more robust guidelines for heat resilience. Although Boston has often addressed mitigation and adaptation as separate problems, Boston's heat report includes policies that take advantage of important feedbacks between climate adaptation and mitigation. Energy retrofits in homes, public housing, and public schools are embraced as a strategy to both reduce building emissions and improve thermal comfort by introducing efficient HVAC systems. The plan also acknowledges that higher temperatures make encouraging biking and public transportation harder, as survey respondents reported that many of the city's streets and corridors lack trees and feel too hot to use in the summer (City of Boston 2022b).

As temperatures warm, Boston will have to reckon with a widespread lack of air conditioning in many homes and workplaces, particularly those that are low-income or have other social vulnerabilities. A city-led survey found that the majority of respondents feel too hot at home when it's hot outside, with heat exposure disproportionately higher in Black and Latino communities (City of Boston 2022b). Numerous schools in Boston and other municipalities in the metro area lack HVAC systems, posing a threat to the health and well-being of children; school districts in Massachusetts have begun to close schools or implement early dismissals because of extreme heat (Shankman 2023). The city has long-term plans to upgrade buildings with energy efficient HVAC systems.

For several years, Boston lagged many other major North American cities in producing an urban forest management plan that incorporates tree canopy in its climate planning. The city commissioned a Tree Canopy Assessment in 2019 (O'Neil-Dunne and Safavi 2019) that tracked changes in tree canopy over the previous five years to understand how Boston's rapid development impacted tree cover. In 2022, the city released an Urban Forest Plan with steps to expand and protect the city's tree canopy over the next two decades as a component of its overall climate adaptation and resilience goals (City of Boston 2022d). The plan has been critiqued by some environmental advocates for not setting measurable targets that the city is accountable for (Bebinger 2022). As most of Boston's recent tree losses occurred on residential land (O'Neil-Dunne and Safavi 2019), restricting tree removal on private property, as well as engaging residents and landowners in tree preservation, could have significant impacts on the overall tree canopy. Boston's City Council recently created an ordinance to help protect trees by placing restrictions on removing trees on public and private property (Soebroto 2023), a strategy recently taken by Cambridge and Newton to regulate tree removal on private land.

These recent steps put Boston on a better path to addressing urban heat, among other benefits. The success of these initiatives will depend on multilevel cooperation with utilities and state agencies. Boston also benefits from learning from advances in neighboring communities. In 2023, Cambridge introduced a "Cool Score," a performance-based standard for site and landscape design that mitigates urban heat through new plantings, shade, cool pavements, and other features (Zoning Ordinance No. 2022-9). Boston could make its own resilience guidelines more explicit to focus on site designs rather than buildings. The city also plans to explore the appropriateness of creating zoning overlay districts for extreme heat (similar to its zoning for sea-level rise) (City of Boston 2022b). Together, the city's proposed strategies will have synergistic effects such as mitigating the urban heat island, reducing greenhouse gas emissions, improving transportation comfort and safety, alleviating energy bills while improving thermal comfort for many residents, mitigating stormwater flooding by building the city's green infrastructure, and addressing environmental inequities.

Equity and Justice

The grossly uneven impacts of climate change among different individuals and communities have prompted scholars, policymakers, and climate activists to call for better attention to equity in climate mitigation and adaptation policy. While inequality infuses social systems on an increasingly global scale, "the city is the scale where questions of justice are felt concretely as part of everyday life" (Marcuse et al. 2009). Moreover, discussions of climate justice, while often focused on global disparities in responsibilities and impacts, have increasingly turned to the urban scale and the question of how climate change responses are shaped by—and may exacerbate—existing inequality (Bulkeley et al. 2014). The environmental justice movement has highlighted deep inequalities in urban landscapes, including the distribution of environmental burdens such as pollution, waste, toxic materials, flood risks, and extreme heat, and of environmental amenities such as access to trees, parks, recreational opportunities, thermal comfort, and transportation. Decades of research has found that this environmental heterogeneity in U.S. cities often falls along lines of race and income, linked to specific policies such as redlining that advance environmental racism and trap certain communities in cycles of disinvestment, poverty, and accumulating environmental burdens. Numerous scholars have also described and critiqued the broader inequities fostered by neoliberal governance in cities over the past several decades, which places "entrepreneurial urbanism" and competitive urban growth has over public interests in shaping urban spaces (While et al. 2004). These already-existing social and economic inequalities in urban experiences can be dramatically exacerbated by climate change. Climate adaptation measures themselves run the risk of perpetuating or exacerbating uneven risks and vulnerabilities among populations, particularly when planning emphasizes "win–win" solutions rather than acknowledging the potential inequities that adaptation interventions may have (Anguelovski et al. 2016). Adaptation actions can result in injustices of omission (such as protecting assets and wealthy communities instead of poor or marginalized people) or through injustices of commission (such as disproportionately displacing poor or marginalized people through adaptation actions) (Swanson 2021).

We can see the impacts of neoliberal governance in the everyday fabric of Boston's recent urban redevelopment, and in Boston's pursuit of economic success through attracting a "creative class" (Florida 2002) while allowing income inequalities to become more entrenched, turning the city into a territory of the already-wealthy rather than an engine of economic mobility. The recent rapid development of Boston's flood-vulnerable Seaport District is a stark illustration of how cities can embrace urban resilience and equity in planning strategies while simultaneously advancing a neoliberal growth agenda that perpetuates high-risk development (Humphries 2025) (Figure 6.1).

Boston's efforts to date also reveal a city that is working to come to terms with the deep inequalities of its past. Like many other major cities, Boston is increasingly building equity explicitly into climate planning, particularly by emphasizing income and racial inequalities among different neighborhoods

Figure 6.1 Waterfront development in Boston's Seaport District has benefitted the city's economy but increased exposure to flooding. Photo by author.

and focusing on vulnerable communities burdened by the impacts of climate change. Urban climate action plans are increasingly drawing on ideas of distributive and procedural justice in framing their responses to climate change; yet they rarely move beyond public engagement to incorporate citizens into decision-making processes (Chu and Cannon 2021). While recent shifts in focus on equity in planning are promising, these plans do not necessarily translate into policies that address existing inequities or ensure equitable climate mitigation and adaptation. These documents tend to focus on immediate equity concerns of different residents rather than considering the longer-term perspective of intergenerational justice that might help to reframe adaptation improvements that create longer-term social problems (Fiack et al. 2021). Monitoring the progress of cities that are adopting equity as a goal of climate action will be important moving forward. However, the metrics for measuring progress on equity are not straightforward.

Boston's previous attempts to integrate equity into climate change governance have been decidedly mixed. In 2015, the city took the innovative step of declaring racial and economic equity as a central pillar of urban resilience; it directed funding from the Rockefeller 100 Resilient Cities program to establishing a Chief Resilience Officer focused specifically on addressing racial equity. Ultimately, however, the city's initial incorporation of urban resilience as a planning concept took two distinct paths, one embedded within the Climate Ready Boston and focused primarily on waterfront resilience, and the other embedded within the Office of Resilience and Racial Equity focused largely on social and racial equity through economic development (Fastiggi et al. 2021; van den Berg and Keenan 2019). In its waterfront adaptation planning, Boston's leaders often expressed a desire to pursue equity without a clear picture of the potential injustices.

The Wu administration has adopted the language of environmental and climate justice into its planning. In addition to the heat planning already described, Boston's urban forest plan includes explicit discussions of distributional injustices in the city's tree canopy, and it incorporates equity concerns in both the distribution of trees and procedural justice of forest planning and tree care and maintenance (City of Boston 2022d), putting it ahead of many urban forest management plans across the United States (Grant et al. 2022). But the operationalization of this planning rhetoric and its impacts are still unclear. A detailed analysis of climate justice-focused policies enacted through the city's BERDO 2.0 building decarbonization strategy suggests that enacting climate justice will be a complex and contested process, and that realizing the broader visions of a just transition will be constrained by the technical and legal requirements of specific policies (Diezmartínez et al. 2024). The formation of a Community Advisory Group described earlier allowed for detailed discussions about how to incorporate justice into policy, and the study found that competing visions of justice shaped even in technical decisions not explicitly associated with environmental justice.

Equity has been an increasing focus of local nonprofit and activist work around climate change adaptation and mitigation. But there are structural challenges to this goal, including the elite nature of climate action networks themselves. A network analysis of the climate adaptation filed in Metro Boston, for example, found that stakeholders lack representative racial diversity and are somewhat siloed into those connected to grassroots groups working on social resilience, and those connected to larger institutions working on physical adaptation (Negrón et al. 2022), pointing to a need to build greater connectivity between stakeholders. A growing number of institutions are including Native perspectives and governance to their climate work, but the roughly 6,000 Native inhabitants in the Greater Boston area are scattered among dozens of tribes, so Native presence in climate justice work is not as organized as in some other urban areas.

Climate vulnerabilities tend to be spread more widely throughout certain neighborhoods, but there are concentrated areas of vulnerability in many neighborhoods of the city (Martin, 2015). Historical lack of investment and loss of trust in city planning in these neighborhoods poses a challenge for procedural and recognition justice in vulnerable communities. In particular, the city will need to foster greater engagement with vulnerable residents, including those with overlapping social vulnerabilities. Boston has demonstrated attention to equity through focusing its climate planning and investments on neighborhoods with high social vulnerability and histories of environmental neglect, such as East Boston. However, in a city with some of the highest real estate prices in the country, Boston's under-invested neighborhoods are also hotspots of gentrification. East Boston has been described as an example of "green gentrification" (Shokry and Anguelovski 2021), though residents and community activists have not always agreed with the characterization of recent green investments as negative (McDonald 2022). While the dangers of green gentrification are not a reason to avoid adaptation investments in vulnerable neighborhoods, they highlight the need for deliberate steps to foster community engagement and procedural justice in neighborhood planning for climate adaptation. The city is currently engaged in a comprehensive planning process to guide development and climate resilience along the East Boston waterfront, which provides an opportunity to incorporate considerations of equity and justice into solutions that address multiple urban challenges, vulnerabilities, and risks.

As described in Chapter 3, Boston's built environment creates variable areas of heat risk, with some of Boston's whitest and wealthiest neighborhoods lie in more vegetated, low-density neighborhoods. Boston has taken promising steps to begin addressing some historical inequities in its built environment that contribute to heat islands, such as using a recent federal grant to study the feasibility of creating a park in Chinatown, a neighborhood that is unfairly burdened with heat and air pollution.(Carlock 2023); improving bus transit, which serves higher proportions of minority and low-income residents (City of Boston 2017a), and supporting renewable energy in lower-income neighborhoods, such as Solarize Eastie, a program to install solar panels and batteries in East Boston. Equity considerations have increasingly been incorporated into major new developments in the city, both in terms of their promised public benefits, and in requirements for diversity in contracting and hiring. These kinds of policies can be applied to climate mitigation and adaptation efforts to ensure that employment and other community benefits are equitably distributed.

Turning these specific policies into a broader "just transition," requires cities to align their policies with both larger-scale state and national policy goals as well as with local environmental justice communities (McKendry 2016). Massachusetts first created a statewide policy around environmental justice in 2002, and a 2014 Executive Order established an environmental justice mandate in state government to protect vulnerable residents from environmental harms. But specific environmental justice policies have been slow to be implemented. An amendment to the state's landmark climate bill in 2021, for instance, established new protections for environmental justice communities and promised to create a special advisory council to review state definitions of and decisions about environmental justice communities, but the council formation was delayed for more than a year (Noor 2022). A new undersecretary for Environmental Justice & Equity, appointed in 2023 under the Healey administration, is a move toward prioritizing justice in state environmental planning and protections. In the state's 2022 Climate Change Assessment, climate impacts are given an "urgency score" that is informed by the disproportionality of exposure for environmental justice populations (Commonwealth of Massachusetts 2022b).

The state's recent steps toward better environmental justice governance may help address environmental inequities across the metropolitan area. In its climate change mitigation and energy transition strategies, the Massachusetts Clean Energy Center has outlined steps that the Commonwealth should take to increase the diversity of its clean energy workforce, including fostering better public awareness of career opportunities and creating workforce development programs that directly reach women and minority workers (Massachusetts Clean Energy Center 2023).

Achieving greater equity in climate change adaptation and mitigation requires addressing broader challenges facing the region, particularly income inequality, housing affordability, and transportation equity. Boston must find new ways to help those left out of the agglomeration economy. In the past, the city has chased new knowledge workers at the expense of others. But the city's human capital includes traditional trades and services that are necessary for maintaining a diverse and flexible economy.

Community resilience through microgrids

A partnership between several community organizations and energy industry representatives has developed solar microgrids in the city of Chelsea and Boston's Chinatown. Led by Resilient Urban Neighborhoods and Green Justice Coalition (RUN-GJC), the partnership focuses on making energy efficiency retrofits and installing clean energy solar panels, batteries, backup generators (Climable, n.d.). They function as a cloud-based network that can provide emergency power in the event of a grid outage, making it more feasible to deploy among smaller and physically disconnected sites. A similar program is being implemented in Chelsea, Massachusetts, and MassCEC has funded feasibility studies for community microgrids in other communities around the state. Although microgrids may not have a major role in reducing overall greenhouse gas emissions statewide, they are gaining popularity among Boston-area communities as path toward local energy resilience and engage environmental justice communities in clean energy. These projects also demonstrate how non-governmental partnerships among a large and diverse group of actors is advancing energy transitions around the city.

Chapter 7

CONCLUSION: LESSONS FOR THE FUTURE

What would a carbon-neutral Boston, if achieved, look like, and what impacts would such a transformation have on urban life? Will sea-level rise and destructive storms eventually force residents to abandon historic neighborhoods? Will increasing heat waves create a public health emergency among populations in the city without access to air conditioning? Will the city continue to thrive or will a climate-stressed future challenge its systems beyond their ability to adapt? Amidst the pursuit of sustainability, carbon neutrality, and resilience in urban planning and policy, we still do not know to what extent such goals are achievable and what kinds of urban conditions they will create. Instead, we are left with discourses about the future driven by urban sociotechnical imaginaries that shape decisions and investment (Tozer and Klenk 2018; Miller 2020). Bostonians have been presented with several visions of the city's climate future. Initial planning for sea-level rise brought several visions of "Living with Water" from Boston's design community, while the Walsh administration published a powerful but vague Resilient Boston Harbor vision that depicted a safe and softly greened version of the city's waterfront, protected by new green space. In campaigning on her Green New Deal platform, current mayor Michelle Wu outlined a vision for Boston's future in distinctly utopian terms, which is worth quoting at length here:

> Imagine the City of Boston leading the way on climate justice. Envision a city where every resident enjoys a healthy home, beautiful public spaces, plentiful local food options, fresh air and clean water, and strong social safety networks. A city with safe and reliable transportation options—including protected infrastructure for cyclists and pedestrians, and fast, frequent, reliable, fare-free transit—that make personal vehicles unnecessary. A city where affordable housing policies keep people in their communities, so that they benefit from green investments in the neighborhoods where they live, without fear of displacement. A city with cultural centers and community gathering spaces, where streets

> are vibrant pedestrian malls and parks host open-air markets and cinemas. It's a city where families can swim and picnic along the banks of the Charles River and pristine Harbor beaches, or walk to beautifully maintained parks and playgrounds in every community. A city where residents never worry about monthly utility costs, because they own the clean energy produced by rooftop solar systems. A hub serving as a global leader in developing new clean renewable energy systems, zero waste, and green technologies. Where Black and brown families share equitably in the prosperity of the city and children attend well-resourced public schools in net-zero, healthy school buildings. Where all residents are protected from sea level rise, flooding, heat waves, and other climate impacts. A new kind of city where poverty, pollution, social and environmental injustices, and racial oppression are rapidly becoming stories from the past. (Wu 2020, 5)

This holistic vision is notable for its inclusion of the various distinct dimensions of urban SETS, including technology and infrastructure; social values of racial and economic equity, safety, and personal autonomy; and the ecological integrity of natural systems. It presents their interactions as mutually beneficial, a kind of sustained harmony that recalls the three pillars of sustainability: economy, environment, and equity. It relies heavily on new infrastructure as the antidote to threats of both environmental and socioeconomic instability. This vision does not acknowledge tradeoffs between temporal and spatial scales of climate resilience, path dependencies, or complex feedback between different interests or interventions. Even Boston, one of the country's oldest cities with some of its longest-lived institutions and infrastructure, can become a "new kind of city." The vision also presents the city as a bounded system in which all these elements and their interactions can seemingly be controlled by good municipal governance. This imagined Boston provides a haven to its residents from economic stress, racism, pollution—even the destabilizing effects of climate change on weather. It overlooks the multiple scales of climate justice (McKendry 2016), including Boston's responsibility as a wealthy city in the Global North to address climate injustices beyond its borders.

Boston's future will be impacted by its own historical development as well as numerous outside forces and global patterns (demographic, social, political, economic, technological) that will shape its adaptive capacity. Even its efforts to address sustainability and climate resilience rely on broader actions. Just five years after publication, the vision of a low-carbon, resilient, safe, and equitable Boston is clouded by federal funding cuts for environmental protections and justice, slowing urban development, and rising inflation.

Boston's long-term future depends on some scientific unknowns in the climate system, such as precipitation patterns, disease ecology, and the melting of the West Antarctic Ice Sheet, which would radically change the footprint of the city and restore many filled areas of land to tidal inundation (Douglas and Kirshen 2022). But it will also be shaped by political, economic, and societal behaviors that are challenging to model. The IPCC has addressed the problem of projecting future societal responses by developing "Shared Socioeconomic Pathways," which provide narratives for how the world may respond to climate change, with resulting implications for emissions, energy and resource use, and land use (Riahi et al. 2017). The SSPs can be used to project how varying demographic and socioeconomic trends and efforts to reduce global emissions and adapt to climate change might impact global systems, including the future of urban growth (Chen et al. 2020). But SSPs have been less useful for telling us what might happen to a particular urban metropolis under the pressures of climate change (Marcotullio and Sorensen 2023). With projected growth, climate risks such as sea-level rise and extreme heat may create new infrastructural pressures and new spatial patterns of settlement and economic investment that exacerbate social inequities, pushing socially vulnerable residents increasingly into areas of risk. Given urbanization trends, the efforts taken today to reduce emissions and to adapt to anticipated climate changes in urban centers like Greater Boston will be critical to creating a future in which the metropolitan area continues to offer a safe, sustainable, and equitable place to live and work for future generations.

As flooding increasingly threatens buildings and neighborhoods of Boston and its nearby communities, municipal governments may lose the revenue from existing real estate and new development that they currently depend on (Shi and Varuzzo 2020). According to a Climate Ready Boston analysis, the city can expect increasingly higher annualized losses from storms in the future: $137 million in the 2030s, $455 million in the 2050s, and $1.39 billion in the 2070s, largely through business interruptions, structure losses, and damage and loss of building contents (City of Boston 2016). Managing and recovering from storms will financially burden the city, making it ever more challenging to rebuild, repair, or adapt as time goes on. A more hopeful scenario is that cities like Boston that have invested heavily in climate planning will be able to command the resources needed to reduce their carbon emissions, revamp their energy infrastructure, and create flood protection systems and other adaptive measures—at least for several more decades. Empirical evidence suggests that coastal urban areas will fortify existing land and eventually encroach on the sea (Esteban et al. 2020), which may lead to "bifurcating coastal futures" with coastal urban areas remaining in place as less-resourced hinterlands depopulate (Lincke and Hinkel 2021, 11).

Uneven urban transformation could pose a challenge for social equity in coastal urban areas. If the trends of gentrification and rising real estate prices continue, it could further push working-class people into higher-risk neighborhoods and resource-poor suburbs. Boston's investments in infrastructure will protect an increasingly elite enclave.

Ultimately, Boston's climate actions to date provide lessons for other cities. Boston has developed a progressive but practical approach to climate change adaptation and mitigation that has allowed it to develop and implement significant policy changes. Its multi-stakeholder planning processes provide a model for moving forward with adaptation proactively and collectively, harnessing multiple actors within the city. But it also provides an example of how challenging it is to overcome the infrastructural and institutional inertia of historic cities, as well as ongoing social and economic inequalities. Boston's Green New Deal represents an attempt to fashion a comprehensive and transformative climate program that includes social equity. By its own metrics, Boston is making steady progress but still falling short of implementing even its short-term goals for 2025, including building coastal resilience projects in its neighborhoods and doubling its building decarbonization workforce (City of Boston 2023). But even if the city falls well short of the full vision of its Green New Deal, the results of its efforts will offer specific policy approaches and pathways for other cities.

One of those lessons, I have argued, is a more integrated approach to managing urban SETS in the face of a changing climate that involves developing municipal frameworks, administrative structures, and policies that bring social, environmental, and technological aspects of the city together. Rather than only seeking synergistic solutions, however, such integration should acknowledge the potential for tradeoffs, feedbacks, and lock-in of maladaptive trajectories in decision-making across SETS domains (Sharifi 2023). In the following sections, I further imagine some ways that Boston could specifically address ongoing challenges.

Innovating Hydrosocial Management

Boston's history of port, industrial, and urban development has shaped its ecological relationships with water and created numerous challenges for a future that will see heavier precipitation and sea-level rise. Numerous stakeholders are working toward a greener and more resilient vision for Boston's rivers, coastal waterfront, stormwater systems. Collectively, these "hydrosocial territories" are complex configurations of infrastructure, ecosystems, people, and institutions (Boelens et al. 2016). Boston has a wealth of talent in design, landscape planning, coastal science, and engineering that can imagine and execute innovative coastal flood protection systems that create new ways of interfacing with rising seas. But if that vision does not expand to encompass the planning, design, maintenance, and governance of a new kind of infrastructure, nature-based flood protection will be limited to small-scale interventions and experiments. Governing urban SETS requires a balance between top-down governance and "bottom-up" experimentation for improving sustainability and resilience (Krueger et al. 2022), as well as flexibility and responsiveness to local events and changes, including public participation in infrastructure design and reorganization (Andersson et al. 2022a). Governing coastal adaptation in Boston Harbor may require creating an institution with the authority to regulate climate adaptation across different jurisdictions and land uses, as well as greater involvement of local communities. Currently, Boston lacks a regulatory environment that promotes innovation and adaptable management on its coasts (Kruel et al. 2018). One potentially powerful tool at Boston's disposal is the public trust doctrine, which is enshrined in Massachusetts law as Chapter 91, sometimes called the Public Waterfront Act. The state has been updating Chapter 91 for coastal resiliency, but attention often focuses on technical regulations rather than rethinking the role of the public trust in protecting public interests as shorelines shift. A proposed new state law (The Mass Ready Act) aims to streamline Chapter 91 permitting for restoration, adaptation, and housing construction in coastal areas, thus attempting to address the twin crises of housing supply and climate change adaptation simultaneously, but it faces pushback from conservation-focused environmental groups wary of continued coastal development.

The city of Boston has harnessed both public and private development to implement coastal protection systems and resilient buildings. This strategy will help protect against gradual sea-level rise and increasing numbers of storms, but continued intensification of extreme weather and storm and tidal flooding over several decades could challenge waterfront areas in new ways. Although managed retreat has been essentially absent from discussions of adaptation in Boston, as the risks and costs of waterfront development grow, we may see a continued trend of diminishing investment in the waterfront, even if the word "retreat" is never used. Eventually, piecemeal decisions about waterfront land use will need to shift to a dedicated strategy. The city and metropolitan area could focus their planning on densifying inland areas at higher ground, anticipating and directing future growth away from the shoreline.

Given its densely built coastal environment, Boston has opportunities to embrace *hybridity* in its infrastructure, developing flexible, adaptive, multifunctional infrastructure to manage coastal risks that shares elements of gray, green, and blue infrastructure (Andersson et al. 2022b). This may include opportunities to integrate coastal protection and stormwater management. Boston's intense focus on waterfront resilience since Hurricane Sandy in 2012 has sometimes overlooked connections between stormwater and coastal flooding, but stormwater flooding will likely be a growing problem in areas of the city and metropolitan area. Boston's new Director of Green Infrastructure represents a positive step toward coordination between Boston Water and Sewer and other agencies. "Green infrastructure" can signify several different types of vegetated features and conceptions (Matsler et al. 2021), but Boston's adopts the relatively narrow US EPA definition of green infrastructure as stormwater management. As a city and metropolitan area facing significant risks from both coastal and inland flooding, the city and its metropolitan areas could seek innovative approaches to water management and adaptation, bridging coastal and inland flood management.

Maintaining Economic Flexibility

Boston's history is marked by economic downturns and reinventions. The city has benefitted from its recent growth, but this growth is driven in part by industries and economic dynamics in biomedical innovation, pharmaceutical development, and health care technology that the city cannot control. Depending on this sector for continued growth and investment makes the city vulnerable as economies change and it leaves the city and region vulnerable to changing federal support for education and health care research and development (Metropolitan Area Planning Council 2021). Economic growth also brings challenges to coastal cities like Boston—including a housing shortage, traffic congestion, gentrification, and a housing affordability crisis—that can undermine social and environmental climate goals. Economic diversity has been an asset to Boston in its past, providing resilience in larger economic shifts, and maintaining economic flexibility will be an important consideration in adaptation to future shocks and stresses.

Cities like Boston are vulnerable to economic losses caused by interconnected climate-related impacts to the physical environment, urban economy, and social fabric (Gasper et al. 2011). Protecting economic diversity—for instance, by preserving zoning and land use regulation that maintain industrial uses against redevelopment pressures—may help to ensure the city's continued flexibility. If Boston is at the precipice of another downturn, we may view its recent development boom as a missed opportunity to bend the city more aggressively to a sustainable, resilient, and carbon-free future. Today, Boston is poised to reinvent itself again by creating a growing workforce devoted to mitigating and preparing for climate change. In this area, as with other sectors where it has excelled, Boston has considerable talent pools to draw from in the metropolitan area, but many workers are not able to afford to live in the city. Local universities have been building new capacities over the past several years in areas related to climate science, energy, and policy. But Boston must continue to foster a political, economic, and regulatory climate that encourages innovation in climate mitigation and adaptation solutions. The city should be a good place to live and work on climate change, not just a place to study it.

In the past, Boston has often pulled itself out of urban problems through major infrastructural interventions: making entire neighborhoods out of marshland, destroying and rebuilding neighborhoods through urban renewal, transforming a polluted harbor into a major recreational and economic asset, plunging a highway underground in the costliest public works project in the country's history. Recent large-scale interventions have required harnessing vast sums from the federal government to "rescue" the city from its problems. Federal politics have changed greatly, and there is no guarantee that the city will be able to receive support for new climate-resilient infrastructure. By maintaining strong partnerships of stakeholders within the city and metropolitan area, Boston will be more likely to harness resources when and where they arise.

Seeking an Equitable Future

Boston has often served as a model for progressive ideals but has fallen short of creating an equitable city for all residents. As Boston again rises to the national and international stage as a progressive leader, this time through the Green New Deal and promises of climate justice, the city must match visions with actions, metrics, and policies that address its deep-running social challenges. Living in Boston is rapidly becoming out of reach for many people, and many of its current residents are heavily burdened by living expenses. If Boston's climate transition contributes to the continued displacement of vulnerable residents, it will ultimately undermine the intended effect of protecting the people who live in Boston today. It is not equitable for a city to address climate vulnerability by pushing its most vulnerable residents out of its borders; therefore, climate justice in Boston cannot be separated from larger issues of housing affordability, transit access, and economic opportunity. If Boston becomes increasingly wealthy, white, well-resourced, and better able to fund adaptation than many of its smaller surrounding communities, the city will become a fortress of resilience in an uneven metropolis. Social inequities will move across borders, with Boston and its wealthier suburbs leaving other communities out of their climate transitions. Operating under an insular view of justice that includes only residents of Boston, the city overlooks its responsibilities to the wider region and to global populations.

Environmental justice and sustainability are increasingly finding convergence, but this agenda is often led by progressive scholars and NGOs and community organizations rather than by governments or private actors (Agyeman et al. 2002). Given the tenuous status of both climate change policy and environmental justice at the federal level, local and state actions in the United States are critical for continuing to advance this agenda. Boston has taken steps to explicitly address issues of racial, social, and economic justice in innovative ways. The city's policies have focused attention on low-income, climate-vulnerable neighborhoods. But it is critical that climate policies help *people*, not just neighborhoods, to avoid creating resilient places for the future elite who will displace current residents. Equitable climate transitions must increasingly consider residents and their capacities, not simply infrastructure. The Green New Deal offers one framework for this transition, but Boston can continue to seek a more equitable and inclusive climate future under other policy frameworks even under future leadership changes.

For example, extreme heat is a problem that affects many of Boston's socially vulnerable residents and formerly redlined neighborhoods. Heat resilience, therefore, is linked to social resilience, and may not be as high an agenda among private consultancies and other actors focused on climate change, while it may also be overlooked by environmental and social service organizations in the Boston area. Governance of urban heat is still nascent and largely experimental in many U.S. cities (Meerow and Keith 2024), but Boston has created an innovative approach to heat resilience that focuses on social equity. Given the uneven access to air conditioning in the Boston area, extreme heat will continue to be an environmental justice issue, as well as a broader climate justice issue as energy demand for air conditioning rises. Boston can pursue heat resilience through thoughtful infrastructural investments and urban greening, but also through programs that foster social connections among vulnerable residents and neighborhoods and improve social care for vulnerable residents during heat waves.

Finding a Metropolitan Balance

As discussed throughout this book, siloed governance and a lack of metropolitan coordination is a challenge for Boston. The city's climate adaptation planning, for instance, has often focused solely on actions within the city's jurisdiction, leaving larger issues of funding, coordination, and regulation as placeholders to deal with in the future (Tu and Yu 2023). Meanwhile, the state's Department of Conservation and Recreation and Department of Transportation are involved in their own studies and plans for coastal flood protection in the city, as is Massport, the regional port authority. A dedicated regional authority for climate resilience would certainly help to coordinate and implement needed infrastructure. But its work would likely focus on a bounded set of projects, such as coastal defense systems, and it would leave the larger metropolitan problems—transportation, housing, and land use—unaddressed. While this certainly follows the Massachusetts playbook, more coordination among the municipalities of Greater Boston on broader climate planning may be necessary. Given the long history of home rule, it is doubtful that Greater Boston will even become a coordinated metropolis. But climate change could lead to new ways of balancing municipal and metropolitan needs.

Coordination can be difficult to achieve when municipalities see little in common. MAPC has played a leadership role in advancing a metropolitan identity, and its Greater Boston Climate Action Plan is a positive step toward greater coordination. But cooperation can also emerge through other kinds of partnerships. The Resilient Mystic Collaborative also offers a promising potential model of collaboration around watersheds. If existing watershed associations were empowered and financially supported to work more closely on resilience, they could provide a model of integrated flood management that considers both precipitation and coastal flood risks, along with other climate-related impacts. With further partnerships and innovative approaches to climate governance, Boston and its neighboring communities can better harness their considerable strengths to ensure a thriving metropolis in the future.

The Future of Urban Systems

I have sought to provide a portrait of the complex and ever-changing urban response to climate change in Boston, rooted in the city's larger historical context. Viewing Boston as an urban social, ecological, and technological system (SETS) highlights the ways that urban history is shaped by interactions between these domains, as well as how past decision-making has often created unintended feedbacks that lead to new urban problems. Boston's current and future climate footprint and risks are shaped by legacy effects of past interactions. Infrastructural and institutional path dependencies impact the city's adaptive capacity and responsiveness to change. Boston's status as a small city within a highly populated metropolis creates mismatches of scale within the larger urban SETS, limiting the ability of the city to reduce its carbon footprint, provide climate-resilient infrastructure, address ecological and public health problems, and advance justice and equity across the entire urban system.

I have described, however, many ways that Boston is working on innovative approaches to address climate change. In particular, the city has benefitted from a political and educational infrastructure that enables strong data collection and collaborative policymaking around climate change. Beyond the individual policies the city has crafted in more than 15 years of climate action, one of the city's most innovative steps has been to implement a broad platform that brings together social, environmental, economic, and infrastructural values and processes. I have argued that this approach is more than a specific set of progressive policies under the Green New Deal; more broadly, it creates new governance structures that integrate aspects of the urban SETS and bring disparate actors together around shared goals. I have also highlighted limits to this integration. By envisioning a future in which SETS interactions are mutually beneficial and guided by a simplistic set of win-win policies and infrastructural investments, Boston's approach to climate governance risks overlooking the need to plan for significant tradeoffs and unintended consequences. As a complex urban SETS, Boston is dynamic and ever-changing, and it requires flexible and adaptive planning.

BIBLIOGRAPHY

Aaronson, Daniel, Jacob Faber, Daniel Hartley, Bhashkar Mazumder, and Patrick Sharkey. 2021. "The Long-Run Effects of the 1930s HOLC 'Redlining' Maps on Place-Based Measures of Economic Opportunity and Socioeconomic Success." *Regional Science and Urban Economics* 86 (January): 103622. https://doi.org/10.1016/j.regsciurbeco.2020.103622.

Abel, David. 2022. "Massport Has a $1 Billion Plan to Cut Climate Pollution. Critics Say It's Nowhere near Enough." *Boston Globe*, March 17. https://www.bostonglobe.com/2022/03/17/science/massport-has-1-billion-plan-cut-climate-pollution-critics-say-its-nowhere-near-enough/.

Agyeman, Julian, Robert D. Bullard, and Bob Evans. 2002. "Exploring the Nexus: Bringing Together Sustainability, Environmental Justice and Equity." *Space and Polity* 6 (1): 77–90. https://doi.org/10.1080/13562570220137907.

Ahlborg, Helene, Ilse Ruiz-Mercado, Sverker Molander, and Omar Masera. 2019. "Bringing Technology into Social-Ecological Systems Research—Motivations for a Socio-Technical-Ecological Systems Approach." *Sustainability* 11 (7): 7. https://doi.org/10.3390/su11072009.

Ahn, D Y, D L Goldberg, Toby Coombes, Gary Kleiman, and S C Anenberg. 2023. "CO2 Emissions from C40 Cities: Citywide Emission Inventories and Comparisons with Global Gridded Emission Datasets." *Environmental Research Letters* 18 (3): 034032. https://doi.org/10.1088/1748-9326/acbb91.

Allain-Dupré, Dorothée. 2020. "The Multi-Level Governance Imperative." *The British Journal of Politics and International Relations* 22 (4): 800–808. https://doi.org/10.1177/1369148120937984.

American Planning Association. 2020. "Sustainable Communities Division Announces the Winners of the Seventh Annual Awards for Excellence in Sustainability." April 27. https://static1.squarespace.com/static/5f8cf739ad8c507bcf1cb83e/t/607608590482c83f2a5e7a81/1618348121741/2020+0427+APA+SCD+Awards+Press+Release.pdf.

Amiri, Ali, Juudit Ottelin, and Jaana Sorvari. 2019. "Are LEED-Certified Buildings Energy-Efficient in Practice?" *Sustainability* 11 (6): 6. https://doi.org/10.3390/su11061672.

Andersson, Erik, Nancy B Grimm, Joshua A Lewis, et al. 2022a. "Urban Climate Resilience through Hybrid Infrastructure." *Current Opinion in Environmental Sustainability* 55 (April): 101158. https://doi.org/10.1016/j.cosust.2022.101158.

Andersson, Erik, Nancy B Grimm, Joshua A Lewis, et al. 2022b. "Urban Climate Resilience through Hybrid Infrastructure." *Current Opinion in Environmental Sustainability* 55 (April): 101158. https://doi.org/10.1016/j.cosust.2022.101158.

Andrew, Brian. 2008. "Market Failure, Government Failure and Externalities in Climate Change Mitigation: The Case for a Carbon Tax." *Public Administration and Development* 28 (5): 393–401. https://doi.org/10.1002/pad.517.

Angelo, Hillary, and David Wachsmuth. 2015. "Urbanizing Urban Political Ecology: A Critique of Methodological Cityism." *International Journal of Urban and Regional Research* 39 (1): 16–27.

Anguelovski, Isabelle, and JoAnn Carmin. 2011. "Something Borrowed, Everything New: Innovation and Institutionalization in Urban Climate Governance." *Current Opinion in Environmental Sustainability* 3 (3): 169–75. https://doi.org/10.1016/j.cosust.2010.12.017.

Anguelovski, Isabelle, Linda Shi, Eric Chu, et al. 2016. "Equity Impacts of Urban Land Use Planning for Climate Adaptation: Critical Perspectives from the Global North and South." *Journal of Planning Education and Research* 36 (3): 333–48. https://doi.org/10.1177/0739456X16645166.

Aylett, Alexander. 2015. "Institutionalizing the Urban Governance of Climate Change Adaptation: Results of an International Survey." *Urban Climate*, Building Capacity for Climate Change Adaptation in Urban Areas, vol. 14 (December): 4–16. https://doi.org/10.1016/j.uclim.2015.06.005.

Bagley, Joseph M. 2007. "A Preshistory of Boston Common." *Bulletin of the Massachusetts Archaeological Society* 68 (1). https://maxwell.bridgew.edu/exhibits/BMAS/pdf/MAS-v68n01.pdf.

Bakhshi, Payam, John Cribbs, Afshin Pourmokhtarian, Justin Steil, Zhengzhen Tan, and Siqi Zheng. 2023. *Public Policy for Net Zero Homes and Affordability*. June.

Banker & Tradesman. 2024. "Editorial: Flooding Regs Generate Developers' Concerns." Banker & Tradesman, February 11. https://bankerandtradesman.com/flooding-regs-generate-developers-concerns/.

Barbier, Edward B. 2010. *A Global Green New Deal: Rethinking the Economic Recovery*. Cambridge University Press. https://doi.org/10.1017/CBO9780511844607.

Barkdoll, Emily. 2021. "Boston Passes Equitable Building Performance Standard." *NRDC*, September 22. https://www.nrdc.org/experts/emily-barkdoll/boston-passes-equitable-building-performance-standard.

Barron, David J, Gerald E Frug, and Rick T Su. 2004. *Dispelling the Myth of Home Rule: Local Power in Greater Boston*. Rappaport Institute for Greater Boston. https://www.mass.gov/doc/home-rule-0/download.

Bassett, Ellen, and Vivek Shandas. 2010. "Innovation and Climate Action Planning: Perspectives From Municipal Plans." *Journal of the American Planning Association* 76 (4): 435–50. https://doi.org/10.1080/01944363.2010.509703.

Basu, Rounaq, and Joseph Ferreira. 2021. "Sustainable Mobility in Auto-Dominated Metro Boston: Challenges and Opportunities Post-COVID-19." *Transport Policy* 103 (March): 197–210. https://doi.org/10.1016/j.tranpol.2021.01.006.

Beauregard, Sandy, Simi Hoque, Paul Fisette, and Benjamin Weil. 2014. "Is Boston Building Better? An Analysis of the Leed Certifiable Standard in the Boston Zoning Code." *Journal of Green Building* 9 (3): 131–50. https://doi.org/10.3992/1943-4618-9.3.131.

Bebinger, Martha. 2022. "Boston's Mayor Wu Announces Investment in Trees for Cooling, Flood Reduction and Beauty." *WBUR*, September 21. https://www.wbur.org/news/2022/09/21/boston-mayor-wu-invests-in-trees-for-cooling-water-savings-and-beauty-climate-change.

Berg, Hanne J. van den, and Jesse M. Keenan. 2019. "Dynamic Vulnerability in the Pursuit of Just Adaptation Processes: A Boston Case Study." *Environmental Science & Policy* 94 (April): 90–100. https://doi.org/10.1016/j.envsci.2018.12.015.

Boelens, Rutgerd, Jaime Hoogesteger, Erik Swyngedouw, Jeroen Vos, and Philippus Wester. 2016. "Hydrosocial Territories: A Political Ecology Perspective." *Water International* 41 (1): 1–14. https://doi.org/10.1080/02508060.2016.1134898.

Bosma, Kirk, Ellen Douglas, Paul Kirshen, Katherine McArthur, Steven Miller, and Chris Watson. 2015. *MassDOT-FHWA Pilot Project Report: Climate Change and Extreme Weather Vulnerability Assessments And Adaptation Options for the Central Artery*. https://www.mass.gov/files/documents/2018/08/09/MassDOT_FHWA_Climate_Change_Vulnerability_1.pdf.

Boston Planning & Development Agency. 2017. "Climate Resiliency Guidance." December 14. http://www.bostonplans.org/getattachment/5d668310-ffd1-4104-98fa-eef30424a9b3.

Boston Planning and Development Agency. 2019. "Coastal Flood Resilience Design Guidelines." September. http://www.bostonplans.org/getattachment/d1114318-1b95-487c-bc36-682f8594e8b2.

Boston Redevelopment Authority. 2010. "Seaport Square to Enhance City's Innovation District with New Innovation Center, 23-Acre Mixed-Use Sustainable Neighborhood." September 21. http://www.bostonplans.org/news-calendar/news-updates/2010/09/21/seaport-square-to-enhance-city-e2-80-99s-innovatio.

Boyle, Alaina D., Graham Leggat, Larissa Morikawa, Yanni Pappas, and Jennie C. Stephens. 2021. "Green New Deal Proposals: Comparing Emerging Transformational Climate Policies at Multiple Scales." *Energy Research & Social Science* 81 (November): 102259. https://doi.org/10.1016/j.erss.2021.102259.

Brooks, Lisa Tanya. 2018. *Our Beloved Kin: A New History of King Philip's War*. New Haven; London: Yale University Press.

Bulkeley, Harriet. 2010. "Cities and the Governing of Climate Change." *Annual Review of Environment and Resources* 35 (1): 229–53. https://doi.org/10.1146/annurev-environ-072809-101747.

Bulkeley, Harriet, Gareth A. S. Edwards, and Sara Fuller. 2014. "Contesting Climate Justice in the City: Examining Politics and Practice in Urban Climate Change Experiments." *Global Environmental Change* 25 (March): 31–40. https://doi.org/10.1016/j.gloenvcha.2014.01.009.

Carlock, Catherine. 2023. "A Park over the Pike in Chinatown? Boston Officials Are Looking into It." Boston Globe, March 22. https://www.bostonglobe.com/2023/03/22/business/stitching-hole-chinatown-with-park-over-pike/.

Carpenter, Stephen R., William A. Brock, Carl Folke, Egbert H. van Nes, and Marten Scheffer. 2015. "Allowing Variance May Enlarge the Safe Operating Space for Exploited Ecosystems." *Proceedings of the National Academy of Sciences* 112 (46): 14384–89. https://doi.org/10.1073/pnas.1511804112.

Chang, Heejun, David J. Yu, Samuel A. Markolf, et al. 2021. "Understanding Urban Flood Resilience in the Anthropocene: A Social–Ecological–Technological Systems (SETS) Learning Framework." *Annals of the American Association of Geographers* 111 (3): 837–57. https://doi.org/10.1080/24694452.2020.1850230.

Chapman, M. G., and A. J. Underwood. 2011. "Evaluation of Ecological Engineering of 'Armoured' Shorelines to Improve Their Value as Habitat." *Journal of Experimental Marine Biology and Ecology*, Global change in marine ecosystems, vol. 400 (1): 302–13. https://doi.org/10.1016/j.jembe.2011.02.025.

Chen, Guangzhao, Xia Li, Xiaoping Liu, et al. 2020. "Global Projections of Future Urban Land Expansion under Shared Socioeconomic Pathways." *Nature Communications* 11 (1): 537. https://doi.org/10.1038/s41467-020-14386-x.

Chester, Mikhail V., Thaddeus R. Miller, Tischa A. Muñoz-Erickson, et al. 2023. "Sensemaking for Entangled Urban Social, Ecological, and Technological Systems in the Anthropocene." *Npj Urban Sustainability* 3 (1): 1–10. https://doi.org/10.1038/s42949-023-00120-1.

Chesto, Jon. 2023. "Fort Point Channel Floodgate Idea Advances, but How to Pay for It?" *Boston Globe*, February 26. https://www.bostonglobe.com/2023/02/26/business/fort-point-channel-floodgate-idea-advances-how-pay-it/.

Childers, Daniel L., Steward T. A. Pickett, J. Morgan Grove, Laura Ogden, and Alison Whitmer. 2014. "Advancing Urban Sustainability Theory and Action: Challenges and Opportunities." *Landscape and Urban Planning* 125 (May): 320–28. https://doi.org/10.1016/j.landurbplan.2014.01.022.

Christensen, Rasmus Corlin, and Rosie Collington. 2024. "New Development: Climate Consulting and the Transformation of Climate Governance." *Public Money & Management* 0 (0): 1–5. https://doi.org/10.1080/09540962.2024.2353672.

Chu, Eric K, and Clare EB Cannon. 2021. "Equity, Inclusion, and Justice as Criteria for Decision-Making on Climate Adaptation in Cities." *Current Opinion in Environmental Sustainability* 51 (August): 85–94. https://doi.org/10.1016/j.cosust.2021.02.009.

City of Boston. 2007. *Climate: Change—The City of Boston's Climate Action Plan.* https://www.boston.gov/sites/default/files/file/2020/02/CAP%202007%20Full%20Report%20Final%2010Jan08%20pdf.pdf.

City of Boston. 2011. *A Climate of Progress—City of Boston Climate Action Plan Update 2011.* https://www.cityofboston.gov/images_documents/A%20Climate%20of%20Progress%20-%20CAP%20Update%202011_tcm3-25020.pdf.

City of Boston. 2014. *2014Climate Action Plan Update.*

City of Boston. 2016. *Climate Ready Boston.* https://www.boston.gov/sites/default/files/20161207_climate_ready_boston_digital2.pdf.

City of Boston. 2017a. "Imagine Boston 2030." July 11. https://www.boston.gov/sites/default/files/embed/file/2018-06/imagine20boston202030_pages2.pdf.

City of Boston. 2017b. *Resilient Boston: A Connected and Equitable City.* https://www.boston.gov/sites/default/files/file/document_files/2017/07/resilient_boston.pdf.

City of Boston. 2019. *City of Boston Climate Action Plan2019Update.*

City of Boston. 2020. *Boston Zero Emission Vehicle Roadmap.* https://www.boston.gov/sites/default/files/file/2020/10/Boston%20ZEV%20Roadmap_1.pdf.

City of Boston. 2021. "City of Boston 2021 Natural Hazard Mitigation Plan Update."

City of Boston. 2022a. "Boston's People and Economy." https://www.boston.gov/sites/default/files/file/2022/04/6%20-Volume%201%20-%20Boston%E2%80%99s%20People%20and%20Economy.pdf.

City of Boston. 2022b. *Heat Resilience Solutions for Boston.* https://content.boston.gov/sites/default/files/file/2022/04/04212022_Boston%20Heat%20Resilience%20Plan_highres-with%20Appendix%20%281%29.pdf.

City of Boston. 2022c. "New Environmental Standards for City Infrastructure Announced." October 21. https://www.boston.gov/news/new-environmental-standards-city-infrastructure-announced.

City of Boston. 2022d. *Urban Forest Plan.* https://www.boston.gov/sites/default/files/file/2023/03/2022%20Urban%20Forest%20Plan%20-%20two%20pages-3.pdf.

City of Boston. 2023. "Green New Deal Dashboard (Beta)." Boston.Gov, May 30. https://www.boston.gov/departments/mayors-office/green-new-deal-dashboard.

City of Boston. 2024. "City of Boston Greenhouse Gas Emissions Inventory, 2005-2022." https://drive.google.com/file/d/1slnHqs9mUeufQi42d_GQ0vbET2Ffs0u4/view?usp=sharing&usp=embed_facebook.

City of Boston. 2025. *Draft Boston 2030 Climate Action Plan—Summer 2025.Pdf.* https://drive.google.com/file/d/1cgs7ByFPVwCNfHzj9Uod5322wEaBNriy/view?usp=embed_facebook.

City of Boston Environment Department. 2021. "Climate Action Fiscal Year 2021 Report." https://www.boston.gov/sites/default/files/file/2021/10/FY21%20Boston%20Climate%20Action%20Report_2.pdf.

City-Business Climate Alliance. n.d. "The CBCA Model." City-Business Climate Alliance. Accessed December 8, 2023. https://www.city-businessclimatealliance.org/the-cbca-model.

Ciurczak, Peter, James Jenning, and Luc Schuster. 2023. *Great Migration to Global Immigration: A Profile of Black Boston.* https://www.bostonindicators.org/-/media/indicators/boston-indicators-reports/report-files/black_boston_profile_page_sm.pdf.

Cleveland, Cutler J, Peter Fox-Penner, Michael J Walsh, et al. 2019. *Carbon-Free Boston.* Institute for Sustainable Energy, Boston University.

Cleveland, John. 2018. "Briefing: How Boston's Green Ribbon Commission Provides Leadership for the City's Climate-Change Strategy." *Life After Carbon*, April 9. http://lifeaftercarbon.net/2018/04/briefing-how-bostons-green-ribbon-commission-provides-leadership-for-the-citys-climate-change-strategy/.

Climable. n.d. "Chinatown Microgrid." Climable.Org. Accessed March 16, 2024. https://climable.org/chinatown-microgrid.

Coffel, Ethan D., Radley M. Horton, and Alex de Sherbinin. 2017. "Temperature and Humidity Based Projections of a Rapid Rise in Global Heat Stress Exposure during the 21st Century." *Environmental Research Letters* 13 (1): 014001. https://doi.org/10.1088/1748-9326/aaa00e.

Cohen, Lizabeth. 2020. *Saving America's Cities: Ed Logue and the Struggle to Renew Urban America in the Suburban Age.* First Picador paperback edition. Picador.

Commonwealth of Massachusetts. 2022a. "Massachusetts Clean Energy and Climate Plan for 2025 and 2030." https://www.mass.gov/doc/clean-energy-and-climate-plan-for-2025-and-2030/download.

Commonwealth of Massachusetts. 2022b. *Massachusetts Climate Change Assessment.* https://www.mass.gov/doc/2022-massachusetts-climate-change-assessment-december-2022-volume-i-executive-summary/download.

Commonwealth of Massachusetts. n.d.-a. "Building Energy Code." Mass.Gov. Accessed March 5, 2024. https://www.mass.gov/info-details/building-energy-code.

Commonwealth of Massachusetts. n.d.-b. "Massachusetts Clean Energy and Climate Metrics." Mass.Gov. Accessed March 4, 2024. https://www.mass.gov/info-details/massachusetts-clean-energy-and-climate-metrics.

Conservation Law Foundation. 2019. *The Massachusetts State Building Code & Climate Change.* https://www.clf.org/wp-content/uploads/2019/03/CLF_ClimateCodeReport_2019.pdf.

Cornelissen, Sharon, and Luisa Godinez-Puig. 2023. "Homebuying Trends in Metro Boston Contribute to New Locations of Racial Segregation." *Joint Center for Housing*

Studies, May 10. https://www.jchs.harvard.edu/blog/homebuying-trends-metro-boston-contribute-new-locations-racial-segregation.

Cromwell, Adelaide. 1994. *The Other Brahmins: Boston's Black Upper Class 1750–1950.* University of Arkansas Press.

Curtin, Daniel J. 2005. "Windfalls, Wipeouts, Givings, and Takings in Dramatic Redevelopment Projects: Bargaining for Better Zoning on Density, Views, and Public Spaces." *Environmental Affairs* 32: 23.

Curwin, Eli. 2023. "New Bill Aims to Reduce Congestion, Fund Transportation Infrastructure." *Boston.Com*, February 10. https://www.boston.com/news/politics/2023/02/10/traffic-congestion-pricing-beacon-hill-could-pass/.

Delmont, Matthew, and Jeanne Theoharis. 2017. "Introduction: Rethinking the Boston 'Busing Crisis.'" *Journal of Urban History* 43 (2): 191–203. https://doi.org/10.1177/0096144216688276.

DeLucia, Christine M. 2018. *Memory Lands: King Philip's War and the Place of Violence in the Northeast.* Yale University Press.

Diezmartínez, Claudia V., Benjamin K. Sovacool, and Anne G. Short Gianotti. 2024. "Operationalizing Climate Justice in the Implementation of Boston's Building Performance Standard." *Nature Cities* 1 (10): 665–76. https://doi.org/10.1038/s44284-024-00121-w.

Dilworth, Richardson, and Robert Stokes. 2013. "Green Growth Machines, LEED Ratings and Value Free Development: The Case of the Philadelphia Property Tax Abatement." *Journal of Urbanism: International Research on Placemaking and Urban Sustainability* 6 (1): 37–51. https://doi.org/10.1080/17549175.2012.692570.

Douglas, Ellen, and Paul Kirshen. 2022. *Climate Change Impacts and Projections for the Greater Boston Area.* Greater Boston Research Advisory Group.

Douglas, Ellen, Paul Kirshen, Robyn Hannigan, Rebecca Herst, and Avery Palaedy. 2016. *Climate Change and Sea Level Rise Projections for Boston.* Boston Research Advisory Group. https://www.boston.gov/sites/default/files/document-file-12-2016/brag_report_-_final.pdf.

Ellison, Katherine. 2024. *Powering Up Together.* The Boston Foundation. https://greenribboncommission.org/document/the-boston-foundation-boston-climate-progress-report-2024/.

Environment Massachusetts Research & Policy Center. 2018. *Shining Cities 2018.* https://environmentamerica.org/massachusetts/resources/shining-cities-2018/.

Esteban, Miguel, Hiroshi Takagi, Laurice Jamero, et al. 2020. "Adaptation to Sea Level Rise: Learning from Present Examples of Land Subsidence." *Ocean & Coastal Management* 189 (May): 104852. https://doi.org/10.1016/j.ocecoaman.2019.104852.

Executive Office of Energy and Environmental Affairs, and Adaptation Advisory Committee. 2011. *Massachusetts Climate Change Adaptation Report.* Commonwealth of Massachusetts.

Faber, Daniel R, and Eric J Krieg. 2002. "Unequal Exposure to Ecological Hazards: Environmental Injustices in the Commonwealth of Massachusetts." *Environmental Health Perspectives* 110 (Suppl 2): 277–88.

Fahey, Ashley. 2022. "What Slowdown in Biotech Spells for Life-Sciences Real Estate Sector." *Boston Business Journal*, June 6. https://www.bizjournals.com/boston/news/2022/06/06/biotech-funding-slowdown-real-estate-impact.html.

Fastiggi, Mary, Sara Meerow, and Thaddeus R Miller. 2021. "Governing Urban Resilience: Organisational Structures and Coordination Strategies in 20

North American City Governments." *Urban Studies* 58 (6): 1262–85. https://doi.org/10.1177/0042098020907277.

Federal Transit Administration. 2022. "Safety Management Inspection—Final Report." U.S. Department of Transportation, August 31. https://www.transit.dot.gov/sites/fta.dot.gov/files/2022-08/FTA-Safety-Management-Inspection-Report-for-MBTA-and-DPU_0.pdf.

Fiack, Duran, Jeremy Cumberbatch, Michael Sutherland, and Nadine Zerphey. 2021. "Sustainable Adaptation: Social Equity and Local Climate Adaptation Planning in U.S. Cities." *Cities* 115 (August): 103235. https://doi.org/10.1016/j.cities.2021.103235.

Fitzgerald, Joan, Michael J Walsh, Sandy Kendall, et al. 2022. *Inaugural Boston Climate Progress Report.* Dukakis Center for Urban and Regional Policy at Northeastern University.

Fitzgerald, Joan, and Julie Wormser. 2023. "Massachusetts Needs a Coastal Adaptation Agency—The Boston Globe." *Boston Globe*, February 28. https://www.bostonglobe.com/2023/02/28/opinion/massachusetts-needs-coastal-adaptation-agency/.

Florida, Richard L. 2002. *The Rise of the Creative Class: And How It's Transforming Work, Leisure, Community and Everyday Life.* Basic Books.

Fontenault, Jeremy, Nathan Vinhateiro, and Kelley Knee. 2013. *Mapping and Analysis of Privately-Owned Coastal Structures along the Massachusetts Shoreline.* Massachusetts Office of Coastal Zone Management.

Gag, Luisa. 2020. *Not on a Shelf: Reporting on the City of Boston's Progress on Go Boston 2030.* Livable Streets Alliance. https://d3n8a8pro7vhmx.cloudfront.net/livablestreetsalliance/pages/6782/attachments/original/1584047644/Go_Boston_2030_report_FINAL.pdf?1584047644.

Gasper, Rebecca, Andrew Blohm, and Matthias Ruth. 2011. "Social and Economic Impacts of Climate Change on the Urban Environment." *Current Opinion in Environmental Sustainability* 3 (3): 150–57. https://doi.org/10.1016/j.cosust.2010.12.009.

Gearino, Dan. 2023. "Massachusetts Just Took a Big Step Away from Natural Gas. Which States Might Follow?" *Inside Climate News*, December 7. https://insideclimatenews.org/news/07122023/massachusetts-natural-gas-ruling/.

Gittman, Rachel K., Steven B. Scyphers, Carter S. Smith, Isabelle P. Neylan, and Jonathan H. Grabowski. 2016. "Ecological Consequences of Shoreline Hardening: A Meta-Analysis." *Bioscience* 66 (9): 763–73. https://doi.org/10.1093/biosci/biw091.

Glaeser, E. 2003. *Reinventing Boston: 1640–2003.* National Bureau of Economic Research. http://www.nber.org/papers/w10166.

Golden, Bill. 2021. "Boston Harbor Regional 'Layered Defense' Coastal Resilience System." EBC Climate Change Webinar Series:, March 16. https://ebcne.org/wp-content/uploads/2020/12/Presentations-Climate-Change-Webinar-Boston-Harbor-Regional-Layered-Defense.pdf.

Gould, Kenneth, and Tammy Lewis. 2016. *Green Gentrification: Urban Sustainability and the Struggle for Environmental Justice.* Routledge. https://doi.org/10.4324/9781315687322.

Grabowski, Z. J., A. M. Matsler, C. Thiel, et al. 2017. "Infrastructures as Socio-Eco-Technical Systems: Five Considerations for Interdisciplinary Dialogue." *Journal of Infrastructure Systems* 23 (4): 02517002. https://doi.org/10.1061/(ASCE)IS.1943-555X.0000383.

Granberry, Phillip, Fatima Aqeel, Michael Endale, et al. 2025. *Boston By the Numbers 2025.* City of Boston.

Grant, Amber, Andrew A. Millward, Sara Edge, Lara A. Roman, and Cheryl Teelucksingh. 2022. "Where Is Environmental Justice? A Review of US Urban Forest Management Plans." *Urban Forestry & Urban Greening* 77 (November): 127737. https://doi.org/10.1016/j.ufug.2022.127737.

Grove, M., Ogden, L., Pickett, S., Boone, C., Buckley, G., Locke, D. H., Lord, C., & Hall, B. 2018. The Legacy Effect: Understanding How Segregation and Environmental Injustice Unfold over Time in Baltimore. *Annals of the American Association of Geographers*, 108 (2), 524–537. https://doi.org/10.1080/24694452.2017.1365585.

Gumprecht, Blake. 2023. *North to Boston: Life Histories from the Black Great Migration in New England.* Oxford University Press.

Gupta, Arpit, Vrinda Mittal, and Stijn Van Nieuwerburgh. 2022. "Work From Home and the Office Real Estate Apocalypse." Working Paper No. 30526. Working Paper Series. National Bureau of Economic Research, September. https://doi.org/10.3386/w30526.

Haglund, Karl. 2003. *Inventing the Charles River.* MIT Press.

Hamin, Elisabeth M., Margaret Ounsworth Steere, and Wendy Sweetser. 2006. "Implementing Growth Management: The Community Preservation Act." *Journal of Planning Education and Research* 26 (1): 53–65. https://doi.org/10.1177/0739456X05285145.

Healey, Maura. 2023. "Healey-Driscoll Administration Launches Statewide Coastal Resiliency Strategy." November 28. https://www.mass.gov/news/healey-driscoll-administration-launches-statewide-coastal-resiliency-strategy.

Heijden, Jeroen van der. 2021a. "When Opportunity Backfires: Exploring the Implementation of Urban Climate Governance Alternatives in Three Major US Cities." *Policy and Society* 40 (1): 116–35. https://doi.org/10.1080/14494035.2021.1934984.

Heijden, Jeroen van der. 2021b. "Why Meta-Research Matters to Regulation and Governance Scholarship: An Illustrative Evidence Synthesis of Responsive Regulation Research." *Regulation & Governance* 15 (S1): S123–42. https://doi.org/10.1111/rego.12378.

Heijden, Jeroen van der. 2023. "Towards a Science of Scaling for Urban Climate Action and Governance." *European Journal of Risk Regulation* 14 (3): 513–25. https://doi.org/10.1017/err.2022.13.

Hendricks, Marccus D., and Shannon Van Zandt. 2021. "Unequal Protection Revisited: Planning for Environmental Justice, Hazard Vulnerability, and Critical Infrastructure in Communities of Color." *Environmental Justice* 14 (2): 87–97. https://doi.org/10.1089/env.2020.0054.

Hillier, Amy E. 2003. "Redlining and the Home Owners' Loan Corporation." *Journal of Urban History* 29 (4): 394–420. https://doi.org/10.1177/0096144203029004002.

Hofstad, Hege, and Trond Vedeld. 2021. "Exploring City Climate Leadership in Theory and Practice: Responding to the Polycentric Challenge." *Journal of Environmental Policy & Planning* 23 (4): 496–509. https://doi.org/10.1080/1523908X.2021.1883425.

Horan, Cynthia. 2009. "The Politics of Competitive Regionalism in Greater Boston." *Journal of Urban Affairs* 31 (3): 349–69. https://doi.org/10.1111/j.1467-9906.2009.00463.x.

Horan, Cynthia. 2025. "Neoliberalizing Infrastructure: Financing Public Transportation in Greater Boston." *Journal of Urban Affairs* 47 (3): 880–99. https://doi.org/10.1080/07352166.2023.2200951.

Hsu, David. 2022. "Straight out of Cape Cod: The Origin of Community Choice Aggregation and Its Spread to Other States." *Energy Research & Social Science* 86 (April): 102393. https://doi.org/10.1016/j.erss.2021.102393.

Hughes, Sara, and Matthew Hoffmann. 2020. "Just Urban Transitions: Toward a Research Agenda." *WIREs Climate Change* 11 (3): e640. https://doi.org/10.1002/wcc.640.

Humphries, Courtney. 2025. "An Urban Resilience Fix: Resolving Waterfront Development and Flood Risks in Boston's Seaport District: Urban Geography: Vol 46, No 7." *Urban Geography* 46 (7): 1497–518.

IPCC. 2022. *Summary for Policymakers. Climate Change 2022: Impacts, Adaptation, and Vulnerability. Contribution of Working Group II to the Sixth Assessment Report of the Intergovernmental Panel on Climate Change.* https://www.ipcc.ch/report/ar6/wg2/downloads/report/IPCC_AR6_WGII_SummaryForPolicymakers.pdf.

Ismay, David, Benjamin Miller, Hong-Hanh Chu, et al. 2020. *Massachusetts 2050 Decarbonization Roadmap.*

Jin, Di, Chris Watson, Hauke Kite-Powell, and Paul Kirshen. 2018. "Evaluating Boston Harbor Cleanup: An Ecosystem Valuation Approach." *Frontiers in Marine Science* 5. https://doi.org/10.3389/fmars.2018.00478.

Johnson, Marilynn S. 2015. *The New Bostonians: How Immigrants Have Transformed the Metro Area since the 1960s.* University of Massachusetts Press. https://www.jstor.org/stable/j.ctt1cx3tdr.

Kaushal, Sujay S., William H. McDowell, Wilfred M. Wollheim, et al. 2015. "Urban Evolution: The Role of Water." *Water* 7 (8): 4063–87. https://doi.org/10.3390/w7084063.

Kennedy, Lawrence W. 1992. *Planning the City upon a Hill: Boston since 1630.* University of Massachusetts Press.

Kim, Minjee. 2020. "Upzoning and Value Capture: How U.S. Local Governments Use Land Use Regulation Power to Create and Capture Value from Real Estate Developments." *Land Use Policy* 95 (June): 104624. https://doi.org/10.1016/j.landusepol.2020.104624.

King, Thomas Hyo-min, and Michael Jemtrud. 2025. *A Strategic Niche Management Framework to Scale Deep Energy Retrofits | Buildings & Cities.* January 10. https://doi.org/10.5334/bc.543.

Kirshen, Paul. 2018. *Feasibility of Harbor-Wide Barrier Systems: Preliminary Analysis for Boston Harbor.* Sustainable Solutions Lab, University of Massachusetts Boston. https://www.greenribboncommission.org/wp-content/uploads/2018/05/Feasibility-of-Harbor-wide-Barriers-Report.pdf.

Kirshen, Paul, Kelly Knee, and Matthias Ruth. 2008. "Climate Change and Coastal Flooding in Metro Boston: Impacts and Adaptation Strategies." *Climatic Change* 90 (4): 453–73. https://doi.org/10.1007/s10584-008-9398-9.

Koop, S. H. A., L. Koetsier, A. Doornhof, et al. 2017. "Assessing the Governance Capacity of Cities to Address Challenges of Water, Waste, and Climate Change." *Water Resources Management* 31 (11): 11. https://doi.org/10.1007/s11269-017-1677-7.

Koppenjan, Joop F. M., and Bert Enserink. 2009. "Public–Private Partnerships in Urban Infrastructures: Reconciling Private Sector Participation and Sustainability." *Public Administration Review* 69 (2): 284–96. https://doi.org/10.1111/j.1540-6210.2008.01974.x.

Krueger, Elisabeth H., Sara M. Constantino, Miguel A. Centeno, Thomas Elmqvist, Elke U. Weber, and Simon A. Levin. 2022. "Governing Sustainable Transformations of Urban Social-Ecological-Technological Systems." *Npj Urban Sustainability* 2 (1): 10. https://doi.org/10.1038/s42949-022-00053-1.

Kruel, Stephanie, Rebecca Herst, and David Cash. 2018. *Governance for a Changing Climate.* Sustainable Solutions Lab, University of Massachusetts Boston. https://www.umb.edu/editor_uploads/images/centers_institutes/sustainable_solutions_lab/Governance-for-a-Changing-Climate-Full-Report-UMB-SSL.pdf.

Kuramochi, Takeshi, Mark Roelfsema, Angel Hsu, et al. 2020. "Beyond National Climate Action: The Impact of Region, City, and Business Commitments on Global Greenhouse Gas Emissions." *Climate Policy* 20 (3): 275–91. https://doi.org/10.1080/14693062.2020.1740150.

Lees, Loretta. 2023. "How Michelle Wu Can Become a Global Mayor on Climate." *Boston Globe*, January 3. https://www.bostonglobe.com/2023/01/02/opinion/how-michelle-wu-can-become-global-mayor-climate/.

Levy, David. 2018. *Financing Climate Resilience: Mobilizing Resources and Incentives to Protect Boston from Climate Risks.* Sustainable Solutions Lab, University of Massachusetts Boston. https://www.umb.edu/editor_uploads/images/centers_institutes/sustainable_solutions_lab/Financing_Climate_Resilience_April_2018.pdf.

Lincke, Daniel, and Jochen Hinkel. 2021. "Coastal Migration Due to 21st Century Sea-Level Rise." *Earth's Future* 9 (5): e2020EF001965. https://doi.org/10.1029/2020EF001965.

Lowery, David. 2000. "A Transactions Costs Model of Metropolitan Governance: Allocation versus Redistribution in Urban America." *Journal of Public Administration Research and Theory: J-PART* 10 (1): 49–78.

Lubber, Mindy, and James W. Hunt. 2010. *Sparking Boston's Climate Revolution.* https://www.cityofboston.gov/Images_Documents/BCA_full_rprt_r5_tcm3-19558.pdf.

Luna, Marcos, and Dominic Nicholas. 2022. "An Environmental Justice Analysis of Distribution-Level Natural Gas Leaks in Massachusetts, USA." *Energy Policy* 162 (March): 112778. https://doi.org/10.1016/j.enpol.2022.112778.

Lundsten, Annie, Atyia Martin, Dallase Scott, Isabella Gambill, and Lindsey Santana. 2023. *Our Shared History: Using Boston's Climate Opportunities to Address Systemic Racism.*

MAPC. 2019. *The Growing Carbon Footprint of Ride-Hailing in Massachusetts.* https://www.mapc.org/wp-content/uploads/2019/07/Growing-Carbon-Footprint-of-Ride-hailing-in-MA.pdf.

Marcotullio, Peter John, and Andre Sorensen. 2023. "Editorial: Future Urban Worlds: Theories, Models, Scenarios, and Observations of Urban Spatial Expansion." *Frontiers in Built Environment* 9 (April). https://doi.org/10.3389/fbuil.2023.1194813.

Marcuse, Peter, James Connolly, Johannes Novy, Ingrid Olivo, Cuz Potter, and Justin Steil. 2009. *Searching for the Just City: Debates in Urban Theory and Practice.* Taylor & Francis Group. http://ebookcentral.proquest.com/lib/bostoncollege-ebooks/detail.action?docID=431793.

Markolf, Sam, Ines ML. Azevedo, Mark Muro, and David G. Victor. 2020. *Pledges and Progress: Steps toward Greenhouse Gas Emissions Reductions in the 100 Largest Cities across the United States.* Brookings. https://www.brookings.edu/articles/pledges-and-progress-steps-toward-greenhouse-gas-emissions-reductions-in-the-100-largest-cities-across-the-united-states/.

Markolf, Samuel A., Mikhail V. Chester, Daniel A. Eisenberg, et al. 2018. "Interdependent Infrastructure as Linked Social, Ecological, and Technological Systems (SETSs) to Address Lock-in and Enhance Resilience." *Earth's Future*, ahead of print, December 10. https://doi.org/10.1029/2018EF000926.

Markus, Maarten, and Federico Savini. 2016. "The Implementation Deficits of Adaptation and Mitigation: Green Buildings and Water Security in Amsterdam and Boston." *Planning Theory & Practice* 17 (4): 497–515. https://doi.org/10.1080/14649357.2016.1210666.

Martin, Jessica, Aja Kennedy, and Luc Schuster. 2025. *Residential Segregation in Greater Boston.* Boston Foundation. https://www.bostonindicators.org/-/media/indicators/boston-indicators-reports/report-files/bi_segregation_073125.pdf.

Mascarenhas, Nina(Nina Theresa). 2020. "Collaborative Governance in Regional Climate Resilience Planning : A Case Study of the Resilient Mystic Collaborative." Thesis, Massachusetts Institute of Technology. https://dspace.mit.edu/handle/1721.1/128969.

Massachusett Tribe. n.d. "We Are The Massachusett—The Massachusett Tribe at Ponkapoag." Accessed December 20, 2019. http://massachusetttribe.org/we-are-the-massachusett.

Massachusetts Clean Energy Center. 2023. *Powering the Future: A Massachusetts Clean Energy Workforce Needs Assessment.* https://www.masscec.com/sites/default/files/documents/Powering%20the%20Future_A%20Massachusetts%20Clean%20Energy%20Workforce%20Needs%20Assessment_Final.pdf.

Massachusetts Department of Energy Resources. 2023. "2023 Technical Guidance: Massachusetts Stretch Energy Codes." September. https://www.mass.gov/doc/2023-stretch-code-technical-guidance-document-main-text/download.

MassDEP. 2019. "2019 Charles Final Fact Sheet." https://www.mass.gov/doc/fact-sheet-for-the-final-determination-to-adopt-a-variance-for-cso-discharges-to-the-charles/download.

Massport. 2022. "Net Zero by 2031." Massport.Com, July 27. https://www.massport.com/environment/roadmap-to-net-zero.

Matsler, A. Marissa, Sara Meerow, Ian C. Mell, and Mitchell A. Pavao-Zuckerman. 2021. "A 'Green' Chameleon: Exploring the Many Disciplinary Definitions, Goals, and Forms of 'Green Infrastructure.'" *Landscape and Urban Planning* 214 (October): 104145. https://doi.org/10.1016/j.landurbplan.2021.104145.

McDonald, Danny. 2022. "Is 'Green Gentrification' Driving Displacement in East Boston? Researchers Say Yes, but Locals Push Back." *BostonGlobe.Com*, April 2. https://www.bostonglobe.com/2022/04/02/metro/is-green-gentrification-driving-displacement-east-boston-researchers-say-yes-locals-push-back/.

McKain, Kathryn, Adrian Down, Steve M. Raciti, et al. 2015. "Methane Emissions from Natural Gas Infrastructure and Use in the Urban Region of Boston, Massachusetts." *Proceedings of the National Academy of Sciences* 112 (7): 1941–46. https://doi.org/10.1073/pnas.1416261112.

McKendry, Corina. 2016. "Cities and the Challenge of Multiscalar Climate Justice: Climate Governance and Social Equity in Chicago, Birmingham, and Vancouver." *Local Environment* 21 (11): 1354–71. https://doi.org/10.1080/13549839.2015.1116064.

McPhearson, Timon, Elizabeth Cook, Marta S-Blá, et al. 2022. "A Social-Ecological-Technological Systems Framework for Urban Ecosystem Services." *One Earth* 5 (May). https://doi.org/10.1016/j.oneear.2022.04.007.

McPhearson, Timon, Christopher M. Raymond, Natalie Gulsrud, et al. 2021a. "Radical Changes Are Needed for Transformations to a Good Anthropocene." *Npj Urban Sustainability* 1 (1): 1–13. https://doi.org/10.1038/s42949-021-00017-x.

McPhearson, Timon, Christopher M. Raymond, Natalie Gulsrud, et al. 2021b. "Radical Changes Are Needed for Transformations to a Good Anthropocene." *Npj Urban Sustainability* 1 (1): 5. https://doi.org/10.1038/s42949-021-00017-x.

Meerow, Sara, and Ladd Keith. 2024. "Cities at the Forefront of Emerging US Heat Governance." *One Earth*7 (8): 1330–34. https://doi.org/10.1016/j.oneear.2024.07.013.

Melosi, Martin V. 2000. *The Sanitary City: Urban Infrastructure in America from Colonial Times to the Present.* Johns Hopkins University Press.

Melosi, Martin V. 2005. "Path Dependence and Urban History: Is a Marriage Possible?" In *Resources of the City.* Routledge.

Menino, Thomas M. 2007. "An Order Relative to Climate Action in Boston." April 13. https://www.cityofboston.gov/images_documents/clim_action_exec_or_tcm3-3890.pdf.

Merino, James A. 1972. "Cooperative Schemes for Greater Boston: 1890-1920." *The New England Quarterly* 45 (2): 196–226. https://doi.org/10.2307/364756.

Metropolitan Area Planning Council. 2021. *MetroCommon 2050*. https://www.mapc.org/get-involved/metrocommon-2050/.

Metropolitan Area Planning Council. 2023. *Water, Water, Everywhere: The Increasing Threat of Stormwater Flooding in Greater Boston.*

Miletsky, Zebulon Vance. 2022. *Before Busing: A History of Boston's Long Black Freedom Struggle*. University of North Carolina Press. https://www.jstor.org/stable/10.5149/9781469662794_miletsky.

Miller, Thaddeus R. 2020. "Imaginaries of Sustainability: The Techno-Politics of Smart Cities." *Science as Culture* 29 (3): 365–87. https://doi.org/10.1080/09505431.2019.1705273.

Mitic, Julia, and Emily White. 2021. "CBCA Interview | 'The Heavy Lifting Starts Now' with the Boston Green Ribbon Commission." *City-Business Climate Alliance*, September 9. https://www.city-businessclimatealliance.org/cbca-knowledge/the-heavy-lifting-starts-now.

Moga, Steven T. 2009. "Marginal Lands and Suburban Nature: Open Space Planning and the Case of the 1893 Boston Metropolitan Parks Plan." *Journal of Planning History* 8 (4): 308–29. https://doi.org/10.1177/1538513209351782.

Mohl, Bruce. 2023. "Maine Jury Delivers Hydro Relief for Mass." *CommonWealth Magazine*, April 20. https://commonwealthmagazine.org/energy/maine-jury-delivers-hydro-relief-for-mass/.

Monstadt, Jochen, Jonas Colen Ladeia Torrens, Mansi Jain, Rachel M Macrorie, and Shaun R Smith. 2022. "Rethinking the Governance of Urban Infrastructural Transformations: A Synthesis of Emerging Approaches." *Current Opinion in Environmental Sustainability* 55 (April): 101157. https://doi.org/10.1016/j.cosust.2022.101157.

Moraff, Ken. 2023. "Stormwater and Green Infrastructure in Boston." Green Infrastructure: Addressing Boston's Stormwater Woes, January 11. https://greenribboncommission.org/wp-content/uploads/2023/01/Green-Infrastructure-GRCx-Webinar_Full-Deck_011123.pdf.

Morgan, Ellyn. 2022. "Statement: New 'Stretch' Energy Code Draft Released by DOER." MAPC, February 11. https://www.mapc.org/news/statement-new-stretch-energy-code-draft-released-by-doer/.

Moss, Timothy. 2020. *Remaking Berlin: A History of the City through Infrastructure, 1920–2020*. MIT Press.

Moura, Paula. 2023. "For EVs to Take off, Boston Needs More Equitable Placement of Chargers." *WBUR*, February 2. https://www.wbur.org/news/2023/02/02/electric-vehicle-chargers-boston.

Nanos, Janelle. 2023. "A 'Doom Loop' Narrative Has Taken over San Francisco. Here's What It Means for Boston.—The Boston Globe." *Boston Globe*, June 24. https://www.bostonglobe.com/2023/06/21/business/urban-doom-loop-in-san-francisco/.

Nardone, Anthony, Kara E. Rudolph, Frosch Rachel Morello, and Joan A. Casey. 2021. "Redlines and Greenspace: The Relationship between Historical Redlining and 2010 Greenspace across the United States." *Environmental Health Perspectives* 129 (1): 017006. https://doi.org/10.1289/EHP7495.

Negrón, Rosalyn, Antonio Raciti, and Rebecca Herst. 2022. *Connecting for Equitable Climate Adaptation*. Sustainable Solutions Lab, University of Massachusetts Boston. https://www.umb.edu/media/umassboston/content-assets/documents/Connecting_for_Equitable_Climate_Adaptation_June_2022.pdf.

Nielsen, Anne Bach, and Marielle Papin. 2021. "The Hybrid Governance of Environmental Transnational Municipal Networks: Lessons from 100 Resilient Cities." *Environment and Planning C: Politics and Space* 39 (4): 667–85. https://doi.org/10.1177/2399654420945332.

Noor, Dharna. 2022. "Mass. Environmental Justice Advisory Council Convenes after Years of Anticipation." *Boston Globe*, February 25. https://www.bostonglobe.com/2022/07/29/science/mass-environmental-justice-advisory-council-convenes-after-years-anticipation/.

Nordgren, John, Missy Stults, and Sara Meerow. 2016. "Supporting Local Climate Change Adaptation: Where We Are and Where We Need to Go." *Environmental Science & Policy* 66 (December): 344–52. https://doi.org/10.1016/j.envsci.2016.05.006.

O'Connell, James C. 2013. *The Hub's Metropolis: From Railroad Suburbs to Smart Growth*. http://www.dawsonera.com/depp/reader/protected/external/AbstractView/S9780262314060.

O'Connell, James C. 2016. "The Legacy of Frederick Law Olmsted's Emerald Necklace in Contemporary Boston." *Fábos Conference on Landscape and Greenway Planning* 5 (1). https://doi.org/10.7275/fabos.641.

O'Neil-Dunne, Jarlath, and Nina Safavi. 2019. *Tree Canopy Assessment: Boston, MA*. Boston Parks and Recreation Department. https://www.boston.gov/sites/default/files/file/2020/09/Change-assessment_w_MJW-letter.pdf.

O'Shaughnessy, Eric, Jenny Heeter, Julien Gattaciecca, Jenny Sauer, Kelly Trumbull, and Emily Chen. 2019. "Empowered Communities: The Rise of Community Choice Aggregation in the United States." *Energy Policy* 132 (September): 1110–19. https://doi.org/10.1016/j.enpol.2019.07.001.

Ostrom, Elinor. 1972. "Metropolitan Reform: Propositions Derived from Two Traditions." *Social Science Quarterly* 53 (3): 474–93.

Pandit, Arka, Elizabeth A. Minné, Feng Li, et al. 2017. "Infrastructure Ecology: An Evolving Paradigm for Sustainable Urban Development." *Journal of Cleaner Production*, Urban ecological infrastructure for healthier cities: governance, management and engineering, vol. 163 (October): S19–27. https://doi.org/10.1016/j.jclepro.2015.09.010.

Patton, Jonathan K. 2014. "Considering the Wet Homelands of Indigenous Massachusetts." *Journal of Social Archaeology* 14 (1): 87–111. https://doi.org/10.1177/1469605313509182.

Phillips, Nathan G., Robert Ackley, Eric R. Crosson, et al. 2013. "Mapping Urban Pipeline Leaks: Methane Leaks across Boston." *Environmental Pollution* 173 (February): 1–4. https://doi.org/10.1016/j.envpol.2012.11.003.

Raifman, Matthew, Armistead G Russell, T Nash Skipper, and Patrick L Kinney. 2020. "Quantifying the Health Impacts of Eliminating Air Pollution Emissions in the City of Boston." *Environmental Research Letters* 15 (9): 094017. https://doi.org/10.1088/1748-9326/ab842b.

Rawson, M. (2010). *Eden on the Charles: The making of Boston*. Harvard University Press. http://hdl.handle.net/2027/heb.30498.

Reilly, Adam. 2020. "Boston's Latest Racial Equity Push Isn't New." Politics. *GBH*, August 3. https://www.wgbh.org/news/politics/2020/08/03/bostons-racial-equity-push-gets-a-restart.

Riahi, Keywan, Detlef P. van Vuuren, Elmar Kriegler, et al. 2017. "The Shared Socioeconomic Pathways and Their Energy, Land Use, and Greenhouse Gas Emissions Implications: An Overview." *Global Environmental Change* 42 (January): 153–68. https://doi.org/10.1016/j.gloenvcha.2016.05.009.

Richardson, Jason, Bruce Mitchell, and Juan Franco. 2019. *Shifting Neighborhoods: Gentrification and Cultural Displacement in American Cities » NCRC*. Research. March 18. https://ncrc.org/gentrification/.

Rosenzweig, Cynthia, William Solecki, Patricia Romero-Lankao, Shagun Mehrotra, Shobhakar Dhakal, and Somayya Ali Ibrahim. 2018. "Pathways to Urban Transformation." In *Climate Change and Cities*, 1st ed., edited by Cynthia Rosenzweig, William D. Solecki, Patricia Romero-Lankao, Shagun Mehrotra, Shobhakar Dhakal, and Somayya Ali Ibrahim. Cambridge University Press. https://doi.org/10.1017/9781316563878.008.

Rudnick, Steven M. 2009. "Cleaning Up After Ourselves." In *Remaking Boston*, edited by Anthony N. Penna and Conrad Edick Wright. An Environmental History of the City and Its Surroundings. University of Pittsburgh Press. JSTOR. https://doi.org/10.2307/j.ctt6wrbm4.7.

Seasholes, Nancy S. 2018. *Gaining Ground: A History of LandmakinginBoston*.

Seavey, Dorie. 2021. *GSEP at the Six-Year Mark*. Gas Leaks Allies. https://www.gastransitionallies.org/gsep.

Seelye, Katharine Q. 2014. "Thomas M. Menino, Mayor Who Led Boston's Renaissance, Is Dead at 71." U.S. *The New York Times*, October 30. https://www.nytimes.com/2014/10/31/us/thomas-m-menino-mayor-who-transformed-boston-dies-at-71.html.

Selig, Kate. 2022. "In Boston's Hottest Neighborhood, Heat Waves Exact a Cost, in the Wallet and on the Nerves." *Boston Globe*, July 23. https://www.bostonglobe.com/2022/07/23/science/bostons-hottest-neighborhood-heat-waves-exact-cost-wallet-nerves/.

Shankman, Sabrina. 2021. "Low-Income Communities Could Be Saving Money on Energy While Helping the Climate, but the DPU Is Standing in the Way—The Boston Globe." *Boston Globe*, December 26. https://www.bostonglobe.com/2021/12/26/science/low-income-communities-could-be-saving-money-energy-while-helping-climate-dpu-is-standing-way/.

Shankman, Sabrina. 2023. "Too Hot to Handle: As Schools Reopen in a Heat Wave, a Warning of the Climate Future." *Boston Globe*, September 6. https://www.bostonglobe.com/2023/09/06/science/opening-in-a-heatwave-massachusetts-schools-strugglea-sign-of-whats-to-come-with-climate-change/.

Shankman, Sabrina, and Emma Platoff. 2023. "Following a Dismal Global Climate Report, Could Massachusetts Push up Its Net-Zero Goal?" *Boston Globe*, March 21. https://www.bostonglobe.com/2023/03/21/science/following-dismal-global-climate-report-could-massachusetts-push-up-its-net-zero-goal/.

Sharifi, Ayyoob. 2023. "Resilience of Urban Social-Ecological-Technological Systems (SETS): A Review." *Sustainable Cities and Society* 99 (December): 104910. https://doi.org/10.1016/j.scs.2023.104910.

Shi, Linda. 2020. "Beyond Flood Risk Reduction: How Can Green Infrastructure Advance Both Social Justice and Regional Impact?" *Socio-Ecological Practice Research*, ahead of print, September 5. https://doi.org/10.1007/s42532-020-00065-0.

Shi, Linda, and Andrew M. Varuzzo. 2020. "Surging Seas, Rising Fiscal Stress: Exploring Municipal Fiscal Vulnerability to Climate Change." *Cities* 100 (May): 102658. https://doi.org/10.1016/j.cities.2020.102658.

Shokry, Galia Shokry, Isabelle, and Isabella Anguelovski. 2021. "Addressing Green and Climate Gentrification in East Boston." In *The Green City and Social Injustice*. Routledge.

Soebroto, Ashley. 2023. "Boston's First Law to Expand the City's Tree Canopy Is in the Works." *Boston Globe*, April 23. https://www.bostonglobe.com/2023/04/23/metro/bostons-first-law-expand-citys-tree-canopy-is-works/.

Sorensen, Andre. 2015. "Taking Path Dependence Seriously: An Historical Institutionalist Research Agenda in Planning History." *Planning Perspectives* 30 (1): 17–38. https://doi.org/10.1080/02665433.2013.874299.

Stanley, Jenn. 2015. "Boston Mayor Names City's First Chief Resilience Officer." *Next City*, August 12. https://nextcity.org/urbanist-news/boston-chief-resilience-officer-announced-rockefeller-100.

Steinberg, Philip E, and George E Clark. 1999. "Troubled Water? Acquiescence, Conflict, and the Politics of Place in Watershed Management." *Political Geography* 18 (4): 477–508. https://doi.org/10.1016/S0962-6298(98)00111-5.

Suarez, Pablo, William Anderson, Vijay Mahal, and T. R. Lakshmanan. 2005. "Impacts of Flooding and Climate Change on Urban Transportation: A Systemwide Performance Assessment of the Boston Metro Area." *Transportation Research Part D: Transport and Environment* 10 (3): 231–44. https://doi.org/10.1016/j.trd.2005.04.007.

Swanson, Kayleigh. 2021. "Equity in Urban Climate Change Adaptation Planning: A Review of Research." *Urban Planning* 6 (4): 4.

Tager, Jack. 1991. "The Massachusetts Miracle." *Historical Journal of Massachusetts* 19 (2). https://www.proquest.com/openview/ecea546fa20f3c6da4ed0c52eb65ad09/1?pq-origsite=gscholar&cbl=1821384.

Tajima, Kayo. 2003. "New Estimates of the Demand for Urban Green Space: Implications for Valuing the Environmental Benefits of Boston's Big Dig Project." *Journal of Urban Affairs* 25 (5): 641–55. https://doi.org/10.1111/j.1467-9906.2003.00006.x.

Tellman, Beth, Julia Bausch, Hallie Eakin, et al. 2018. "Adaptive Pathways and Coupled Infrastructure: Seven Centuries of Adaptation to Water Risk and the Production of Vulnerability in Mexico City." *Ecology and Society* 23 (1). https://doi.org/10.5751/ES-09712-230101.

Tozer, Laura, and Nicole Klenk. 2018. "Discourses of Carbon Neutrality and Imaginaries of Urban Futures." *Energy Research & Social Science*, Energy and the Future, vol. 35 (January): 174–81. https://doi.org/10.1016/j.erss.2017.10.017.

Trustees of Reservations. n.d. "Piers Park III, East Boston." One Waterfront. Accessed March 4, 2024. https://onewaterfront.thetrustees.org/pp3.

Tu, Shin, and Siyu Yu. 2023. "Urban Planning for Climate Change: Comparing Climate Adaptation Plans between Taipei and Boston." *Sustainability* 15 (2): 2. https://doi.org/10.3390/su15020934.

U.S. Global Change Research Program. 2023. "Fifth National Climate Assessment." In *Fifth National Climate Assessment*. U.S. Global Change Research Program, Washington, DC. https://nca2023.globalchange.gov/.

Valdez, Anna. 2020. "Listening to Greater Boston's Climate Change Concerns." University of Massachusetts Boston. https://www.proquest.com/openview/89b80eed7408f58f050c15fc0adf155a/1?pq-origsite=gscholar&cbl=51922&diss=y.

Van Voorhis, Scott. 2021. "Industry Groups Worry Massachusetts Climate Bill Could Derail Development." *Engineering News Record*, January 6. https://www.enr.com/articles/50957-industry-groups-worry-massachusetts-climate-bill-could-derail-development.

Vaznis, James. 2023. "Boston Now Spends More per Student than Any Other Large School District in the Nation." *Boston Globe*, May 30. https://www.bostonglobe.com/2023/05/30/metro/boston-now-spends-more-per-student-than-any-other-large-school-district-nation/.

Viall, Tim. 2023. "Greater Boston Climate Action Plan." *MAPC*, October 24. https://www.mapc.org/resource-library/metro-boston-regional-climate-action-plan/.

Vicinity Energy. 2021. "Electrifying District Energy in Boston & Cambridge." Vicinity, September 27. https://www.vicinityenergy.us/blog/path-to-greener-future-electrifying-district-energy-boston-cambridge.

Vrabel, Jim. 2014. *A People's History of the New Boston*. University of Massachusetts Press.

Walsh, Mayor Martin J. 2019. "An Order Relative to Municipal Carbon-Neutral Buildings in Boston." October 11. https://www.boston.gov/sites/default/files/file/2019/12/201912111141.pdf.

Warner, Sam Bass. 1978. *Streetcar Suburbs*. Harvard University Press. https://doi.org/10.2307/j.ctvjsf66f.

Wheeler, Stephen M. 2008. "State and Municipal Climate Change Plans: The First Generation." *Journal of the American Planning Association* 74 (4): 481–96. https://doi.org/10.1080/01944360802377973.

While, Aidan, Andrew E. G. Jonas, and David Gibbs. 2004. "The Environment and the Entrepreneurial City: Searching for the Urban 'Sustainability Fix' in Manchester and Leeds." *International Journal of Urban and Regional Research* 28 (3): 549–69. https://doi.org/10.1111/j.0309-1317.2004.00535.x.

Wild, Kirsty, Alistair Woodward, Adrian Field, and Alex Macmillan. 2018. "Beyond 'Bikelash': Engaging with Community Opposition to Cycle Lanes." *Mobilities* 13 (4): 505–19. https://doi.org/10.1080/17450101.2017.1408950.

Wise, R. M., I. Fazey, M. Stafford Smith, et al. 2014. "Reconceptualising Adaptation to Climate Change as Part of Pathways of Change and Response." *Global Environmental Change* 28 (September): 325–36. https://doi.org/10.1016/j.gloenvcha.2013.12.002.

Woerner, Stephen, and Robert Rio. 2022. "National Grid Has New Vision for Heating." *CommonWealth Magazine*, April 19. https://commonwealthmagazine.org/energy/national-grid-has-new-vision-for-heating/.

Woodruff, Sierra, Sara Meerow, Philip Gilbertson, et al. 2021. "Is Flood Resilience Planning Improving? A Longitudinal Analysis of Networks of Plans in Boston and Fort Lauderdale." *Climate Risk Management* 34 (January): 100354. https://doi.org/10.1016/j.crm.2021.100354.

Wu, Michelle. 2019. *Fixing Boston's Broken Development Process: Why and How to Abolish the BPDA*. https://assets.ctfassets.net/1hf11j69ure4/4jCdriPnGOtb9gpBvNjqUj/34da92377c5112083e0c998e844589f7/abolish-bpda.pdf.

Wu, Michelle. 2020. "Planning for a Boston Green New Deal and Just Recovery." August. https://assets.ctfassets.net/1hf11j69ure4/B6NLxlOVxTVMNbHEvFaQE/700f4762bae92990f91327a7e01e2f09/Boston-Green-New-Deal-August-2020-FINAL.pdf.

Young, Lance. n.d. "From Paradise to Prison." *Partnership of Historic Bostons*. Accessed January 13, 2024. https://historicbostons.org/blog-1/deer.

Zehngebot, Corey, and Richard Peiser. 2014. "Learning from Boston and Other Innovators." *Planning*.

INDEX

www.ingramcontent.com/pod-product-compliance
Lightning Source LLC
LaVergne TN
LVHW102108101026
849885LV00029B/127